NLP—
The Power of
Sensory Preference

People tend to experience the world through one of three senses: sight, sound, or feeling. They emphasize one of the three more than the others. Through their preference, they become known as visual, auditory, or kinesthetic types. And when you have the ability to diagnose another person's sensory preference (through breathing patterns, eye movements, and language), your knowledge becomes power...

Rapport technology teaches you to:

UNDERSTAND SENSORY PREFERENCE CUES in yourself and other persons to enhance your influence over them.

MATCH YOUR STYLE to that of others. When you use NLP mirroring techniques, people will immediately find you more persuasive, compatible, and attractive.

USE SPECIAL ANCHORING WORDS, SOUNDS, AND GESTURES to affect the emotions and judgment of people around you.

Arm yourself with knowledge. You'll achieve...

Instant
Rapport

Instant Rapport

MICHAEL BROOKS

WARNER BOOKS

A Time Warner Company

Copyright © 1989 by Michael Brooks
All rights reserved
Warner Books, Inc., 1271 Avenue of the Americas, New York, NY 10020

Visit our Web site at http://warnerbooks.com

w A Time Warner Company

Printed in the United States of America
First trade printing: May 1990

20   19   18   17   16   15   14

Library of Congress Cataloging-in-Publication Data

Brooks, Michael.
  Instant rapport.

  1. Interpersonal relations.   2. Nonverbal
communication.   I. Title.
HM132.B745   1989   302.3'4   88-27702
ISBN 0-446-39133-6 (pbk) (U.S.A. and Can.)

Book design: H. Roberts
Cover design: Anne Twomey

For Mom...
To the memory of my Father...
And for Shoshone Longfellow

Acknowledgments

When I first began this project a few years ago, it seemed to me that the process of writing a book on a subject yet to be explored by a major publisher would take no less than a totally committed campaign to succeed. My assumption proved to be quite accurate.

This book would never have come to pass without the champion of its cause, my literary agent and friend, Alfred (The Lionhearted) Lowman. He literally sourced the power for the better part of the process, and encouraged me all the way through it. Thank you, Al. I am in your service.

My editor, Leslie Keenan, worked tirelessly refining points and clarifying issues that added greatly to the explanation and value of the material. She forced me to insist on the best of myself while supporting me at those times when I needed encouragement. Thank you, Leslie, for your contribution to this book. And thank you for being my friend.

I am grateful to John Grinder and Richard Bandler for conceiving the model of NLP.

Thanks to Brian Moore for handling so many details with integrity and responsibility, and for handling me with kid gloves.

Cathy Carapella gave of her time graciously, very competently assisting me in manuscript production—usually in emergency situations. Chaya Koprak did a wonderful job designing the eye accessing cue diagrams. Barry Kaplan, Bob Mansdorf and Lee Wecker as well as Rev. Katherine Henderson encouraged me; and Geoff Minte gave more than his share of kindnesses. And, of course, Billy Miller who supported this campaign both in deed and in kind.

I would like to thank my publisher, Nansey Neiman, who gave me this unique opportunity in the first place; and a special thank you to Ling Lucas for her demonstration of confidence. Additionally, my grateful thanks to Jim Frost, Jackie Meyer, Harvey-Jane Kowal, Kate Wheble and everyone at Warner who worked so hard to bring this book to fruition.

Sometimes in life, one must lose someone very special to open the forum for self-discovery. I was quite fortunate to have once had and then lost such a highly excellent person.

Contents

Author's Note

In this book, the pronouns "he" and "she" are used interchangeably. Examples are given throughout using both genders equally. Nothing should be inferred about the characteristics of certain types to either sex.

instant (in' stænt) *adj*. immediate, direct, current. A moment in time. An infinitesimally quick moment of now.

rapport (rå pôr') *n*. a harmonious, empathetic, or sympathetic relation or connection to another self. An accord or affinity. In an ecological alignment with another system. *Fr*. rapporter: to offer back with grace and elegance. *en rapport*.

Instant
Rapport

INTRODUCTION

ROM time to time in life, and not very often at that, a fortunate few of us chance upon something so new and inspiring, and with such credibility, that for a moment we're shocked into questioning its very existence. But then, when we get past our initial surprise, we think, "This is really quite amazing. How come I've never heard about it before?"

Such was the question I asked myself over and over when I first discovered neurolinguistic programming. Trying to find information about it was almost impossible. No one seemed to know anything. Doubts flew into my head: "Maybe I'm wrong. Maybe this isn't as good as it seems. Could such a remarkable technology have been neglected for so long? And if so, why?"

Thankfully, my discovery turned out to be one of those good things in life that just hadn't been talked about very much. In fact, neurolinguistic programming, or NLP as it's called, was not only a discovery that was hard to come by—indeed, I must confess I rather gracelessly collided with it—but was also something its practitioners seemed to talk about... how shall I put this?... almost reluctantly. Not that I could find many devotees. In fact, as time went on, I realized that NLP was either not very well known or was something its students weren't thrilled about sharing. I eventually learned that both were the case. I really can't say with certainty for which of these reasons my curiosity was piqued; probably it had to do with all of them. This much I knew for certain: I had haphazardly uncovered something that seemed immensely valuable; something powerful yet simple in application, and something as yet virtually unknown. A voice within shouted, "You've made a discovery!" I didn't have the awareness then to know that this was not going to be an easy road. But I was virtually compelled— even driven—to find out more about this thing; this miracle looking for a reason to happen. Being the persistent child of intention I have always been, I was extremely motivated to master this wonderful new science. And I did that. But, one enlightening day, I realized that it wasn't all of NLP that was useful, not by any means. It was the part of it where its motor would be; one part, out of many, which was the essence of true power. A part, which I've written about—and which you hold in your hands presently—which represents the very key to true charismatic, persuasive and personal power: the power of rapport.

Instant Rapport is a book and methodology that will allow you to remake the way the world perceives you. It will change people's experience of you so that barriers dissolve away. It will make you a powerful person to be with and talk to, share time with, and love. It will allow you to eliminate those self-limiting dialogues you carry in your head that prevent you from successfully influencing others, and it will free up energy to create new levels of personal accomplishment. If you want to change and shake loose from the effort that's required to communicate with others,

Instant Rapport and the technology it embraces, is for you. It will provide you with a way out of the "pea soup" of everyday chatter. This technology is unique and so effective that your everyday life will be more rewarding, your relationships will take on new freshness, and your ability to handle the problems of life will be enhanced exponentially.

In *Instant Rapport*, we'll learn and examine the techniques of rapport-dynamics and NLP and how their use will make it possible for us quickly to gain rapport with others; to have others understand us with unheard-of clarity, so that we truly enjoy the relationships we have; to live happily ever after with someone we love but just couldn't make it with before; and to achieve understanding and feelings of certainty with others.

Using rapport-technology will enable you to develop long-lasting and total rapport and:

• Significantly improve and complete your relationships with others—especially significant others, such as your lover, your family members, your boss, your peers, your customers, your clients, and your friends.

• Remove a good deal of the nervous energy you spend in communicating ineffectively, thereby making your presentation elegant and compliable.

• Communicate better, and on the most personal level, with others as well as with yourself, which will allow you to let go of unwanted behaviors and to develop personal excellence.

• Be *very* persuasive, influencing and building rapport with people as you easily overcome their resistance in a way you never have before. You will be empowered to communicate with impact.

Rapport-technology is not about how the universe works. Nor is it an absolute or singular truth. Rapport-technology *is* a model—one with a very sophisticated and dynamic approach to supereffective communication. It explains the way people experience and perceive their world, then teaches you to reach them using *their* specific patterns of perception, so that you are totally and clearly understood. Some people refer to this as "being on the same wavelength."

Rapport is experiencing the world through the same portal as the person you're communicating with. It's speaking the same language, even when you don't necessarily understand each other's words. In fact, rapport doesn't require understanding! Being in rapport is miraculous because it opens up whole new worlds of behavioral possibilities, opportunities, and relationships, thereby creating that which heretofore has been unattainable. Sharing rapport is like jumping inside another's nervous system and suddenly understanding the way they make sense of reality. It's truly being able to make others' points of view your own *and* having them accept your point of view *as their own*. It's traveling down the same road. Do you remember how terrifically the lion, the tin man, and the scarecrow communicated once they truly understood that they had a common purpose? The first thing that happened was mutual support. They each understood how important it was for the others to make it to Emerald City. It *served* them to be in rapport. And in fact, had they been unable to create rapport rather quickly, they most likely wouldn't have gotten any farther than the haunted forest. Rapport is just like that.

Without rapport, life doesn't work. Literally. When you go to work, you work against the flow. Your boss becomes a horror to be with, your assistants don't understand what you're saying, and you don't engage your clients. When you come home, your relationships suffer. Your mate is hard to live with, miscommunication is the order of the day, and sharing—that part of relating which binds all others—is next to impossible. Living without rapport is throwing sand in the face of life; you don't get what you want, because you're unable to relate.

If you have ever experienced rapport—that moment in

the course of your daily life where a look of the eye, a turn of phrase, or the touch of a hand has put you in total rapport with another person—you will immediately understand the significance of rapport-technology. We've all experienced this phenomenon from time to time, yet few of us know we have access to this natural ability and can produce it at will. Rapport conditioning is a skill, one that we learn from our first moments of life, and, like any other learned skill, it can be developed, enhanced, and refined. Rapport-technology is about getting in touch with that part of ourselves and tapping in to it on demand, regaining the ability to bond instantly with others.

I developed rapport-technology using the model and discoveries of NLP. The two are very closely related. In fact, NLP talks about rapport and treats it as a cornerstone in human relations. But NLP, in its very attempt to explain rapport, ignores the enormous miracle rapport can manifest in society. It becomes self-centered, content to exist for the purpose of its own examination. It falls into a category that Dale Carnegie referred to as "day-tight compartments": mired in its own perpetuation, NLP steers away from life and the living and toward empirical, fluffy self-aggrandizement. Like a child in the forest, it loses its way. I chose to extract that part of NLP which can work for us, right now, and explain it in such a way that it becomes available for the creation of rapport. I ask, what good does knowing meta theory, unspecified TOTE's, and Outcome Sequitur do for those of us miserable in our petard of loneliness and alienation? As far as I'm concerned, let's take the good stuff, simplify it, and make it elegant enough that all of us can use it. If Euclid's wonderful and brilliant treatment of geometry never got to those who could make use of it—to those who design our bridges and build our shelters—what inherent good would it be? Since I was unwilling to make use of a model that couldn't be transformed to an appealing, getatable process, it was a natural progression for me to find a way in which I could deliver that part of NLP theory which I had certainty about—and, even more to the point, which I knew would contribute to the quality of people's lives.

My first blush with NLP came about as a result of blind luck. I had reached a plateau in my life, a time of reevaluation. I had been pretty successful in my endeavors, both in my work and my pastimes. I started out my adult life as a psychologist, a social scientist committed to the study, diagnosis, and treatment of diseases of the spirit. Modesty aside, I was good at this, and it provided me with a reason for being. I enjoyed the work, too, for it gave me the opportunity to exercise my affinity with people while enabling me to stretch intellectually. Toward the end of my psychological career, I had taken very much to the study of cognitive styles, that branch of clinical work devoted exclusively to the way thought influences feeling. It was this subject that would lead, years later, to my inadvertently finding NLP.

Then, through an odd turn of events, I found myself involved in all sorts of entrepreneurial endeavors, financing various projects while acting as a consultant to others. In a very short time, I became first financially secure, then well-to-do. It was a time of good fortune for me, monetarily. But at the same time, I was suffering emotionally. I had begun to lose my *joie de vivre*, putting the travails of business before all else in my life. I didn't know it at the time, but I was also losing my humanity, as it were. I was slowly murdering life and not taking responsibility for it.

My relationships began to deteriorate, and though I struggled valiantly to maintain them, they became elusive and alien. I began to feel isolated and disassociated from those I had been very close with, even my fiancée. I grew terribly discontent—and after a while angry—at my inability to effect change. While having the most wonderful rapport with her, I was out of rapport with who I was. From all this space of uncertainty, a cavernous emptiness grew inside me, an idle despair that so incipiently overtook me, then us, that in the Christmas of that year, I lost not only her and our life together, but myself and my resources. Within a period of two months, I was alone, broke, and without a strategy for living. In short, I was devastated.

I lost pretty much everything I had; certainly everything that meant something to me. As easily as I was heretofore able to produce and create, I now, even more easily, destroyed. The residue from that two-month period followed me for the better part of a year. During this time, things got progressively bleaker. I lost twenty-five pounds, looked awful, and felt worse. One by one my "friends" and acquaintances stopped calling. My old girlfriend, who had been so very close to me for so long, watched me go through this from afar, yet didn't reach out. In fact, as if to put icing on the cake, she got married. If I recall correctly, her wedding took place the week our country home went into foreclosure. Not being able to find surcease, I wandered through this part of my life a forlorn scrap of previous brilliance, a forsaken almost-human, until, I now deduce, I had gotten enough punishment to satisfy whatever karma I had created.

I undertook a journey of renewal. I mustered whatever reinforcements I had left and began to investigate everything, especially as it pertained to relationship and communication. If it was published or talked about, I studied it. I was ravenous to learn. It was while I was rereading Jung and Titchner that an article caught my eye, something about how we represent experience to ourselves; the way we see the world. It was then that a light began to blaze for me at the end of a very dark tunnel; one that would erupt into the warming sun of discovery. But my work had just begun.

And it *was* work. Just finding the authors' references proved to be a monumental task. And when I did finally locate them, they led nowhere. Finally, after months of investigative research, I found a book written in lecture form taken from an obscure seminar done by the author some few years before. It was fascinating. I must have read it a hundred times before locating yet another of these books, written in the same hard-to-follow but enchanting style. It was then that I started asking myself, "Why would anyone possessing such wonderful knowledge not aggressively seek to give it to the world?" I simply didn't understand that at all.

Months and months passed, while I uncovered the odd book here, an old manuscript there. About a year into it, I actually found a place that claimed to be an institute devoted to the teaching of these new techniques. But when I went there, it wasn't at all what it claimed to be. It was strange. Instead of an enlightened fortress teeming with inspired and motivated people, I found an eerie little dump, poorly lit, harboring promises of expertise for an *outrageous* price. We're talking thousands and thousands of dollars here! And devotion to duty? You really had to be willing to make a lifetime commitment to become "certified." Except no one knew what being certified meant. There was no regulating body or state board of examiners, nor was there any higher authority. You worked and slaved and paid, (the key word here is *paid*) only to be doled out a few tiny morsels of information now and then. It was unbelievable. When I met the "director" of this place, I felt as though I should take *her* under *my* care. I soon realized this was not the Emerald City I thought it would be, and I set out once again on a journey fraught with more frustration to find what I hoped would be Oz.

A year went by, during which I managed to unearth some few hundred books, monographs, discarded lecture notes—even a videotape of the brilliant therapist Milton Erickson, M.D., who spoke elegantly about the nature of experience. Unfortunately, Erickson had recently passed on, and I had no luck in locating a disciple. All of these sources presented me with an inscrutable and oftentimes enigmatic shell of NLP. But I continued studying this subject for well over a year and a half and became quite knowledgeable. Yet, I wanted someone to train with, someone to help me carve out my own ideas, as these were now crystallizing in my brain. I was restless in my search for more data. I knew I had truly found a miraculous technology, literally collecting cobwebs somewhere on discovery's shelf, and I was determined to find a way to share it with the world. It would have been unconscionable to sweep something this wonderful under the proverbial rug. Yet, I could also see that unless it was translated and broken down to a more digestible form, it would never be palpable or palatable enough to be attractive to the masses. But what could I do? I needed more time. More work. And an angel to supply a few answers.

Because of my investigative obsession—in some ways, as I now think back, I had become akin to the mad scientist of the movie thrillers—I hadn't been noticing how my life had changed. I hadn't stopped long enough to take a breath. If I had, I would have been quite perplexed at the new people who had entered my life. I suddenly found myself with new and lovely friends. And there were others—students, sort of—who liked where I was and were as entranced as I by the work I was doing. But even these friends paled when compared with my new best friend. I don't remember exactly when he started to hang around, but it was joyful to have him there. With the quizzical look of puzzlement on my face, I would now and then stop what I was doing, lie back, and sort of bask in the delight he brought simply by being there.

You see, he was me.

I had found myself after losing myself, and my rediscovered self was someone I really liked, again. And then a funny thing happened. People started liking me even more, and my level of connection with those in my life, and those new to my life, raised itself by an order of magnitude. My clarity of self-expression improved. I lightened up and started to smile again. I began to effect change in my life. I was experiencing a perceptual shift at a level I had never before thought possible. But most of all, I found myself. And through this genesis, this rebirth, I couldn't help but be conscious of a new attitude I had. It was an attitude of not possessing an attitude. And because of this, I was relating to people in a new and effortless way. Even those to whom I didn't relate started relating to me. And then one day I knew my work and effort and toil and tears had begun to pay off. I was alive again.

It was through this new relationship with myself that I discovered what had so revitalized me. I knew it had to be more than NLP alone; it had to be something that made me "fit" better, something that made me terrific for others to be with. And then simply, with no great fanfare, I realized what it was. It wasn't that people were so attracted to Michael Brooks or who he was. Or how nice looking or smart he might be. Or even the interesting facts of the soap opera of his life. No, it wasn't that at all. People wanted to be with me because I reminded them of themselves. People liked me because I was like them. I had so learned the new technology that I had been using it continually as an extension of myself, but in a context that *reflected other people's qualities, peculiar to them, individually*. It didn't work like I had thought it would; it just worked. I didn't have to "do" anything, which at first bothered me. There was no more technique involved. It had become a process, and the process was me. I was able to have instant rapport with just about anybody. In the past, I wasn't able to *have* rapport. It was something that just occurred once in a while, sort of like discovering a ten-dollar bill on the sidewalk. Terrific to find, kind of miraculous, really, but nevertheless something one doesn't count on happening again. Rapport was exactly like that. I couldn't control its behavior. Have you ever noticed how people treat the appearance of rapport? It sort of "happens" to us. Kind of like this "thing," which has a mind of its own, that materializes outside our sphere of influence. It's as though we don't want to take responsibility for enjoying rapport because we're erroneously convinced that we have no control over it. We usually consider ourselves totally at the mercy of rapport—not a creator of it.

As a natural expansion of my work, I began talking to more and more people, in larger and larger groups. Restaurants became living rooms that became lecture halls. And as I met all these new friends, and saw miracle after miracle, I truly became convinced that rapport-technology was something I had no choice but to share.

My initial resistance to writing about it was born of the fear that knowledge of the process might be used unethically. You see, rapport-technology is extremely powerful, and the methods revealed in any exposé would lend themselves to possible misuse, if only as a result of insufficient training. Like karate, the most dangerous exponent of this art would be its least educated practitioner. Nonetheless, it just didn't sit right with me, leaving such a magnificent discovery to gather dust somewhere in humanity's attic. I was compelled to write about it, to get it to as many people as I could. This book is the result of that quest.

People suffer from a lack of rapport in their lives. Until now they have been denied the use of an informative data base dedicated to the subject of building rapport. Although many contemporary books have been written with the intention of being a vanguard to attaining happiness, they have, by and large, missed their mark. They divide themselves, hopelessly, into two groups: those that focus on sympathy and commiseration but are devoid of the strategies of what actually to *do* to effect change, and those that concern themselves with methodology, such as astrology, body language, or even psychotherapeutic techniques, which offer a system or remedy but are not "real." They address themselves with "fluffy" notions and theories that even the most ardent devotees have trouble applying to everyday life. Moreover, they leave out the necessary component of empathy. Neither one of these is able to incorporate the necessary criteria of the other. *Instant Rapport* offers the best of both worlds: "high-tech" *and* "high-touch"—a highly understandable system that *really works*, wrapped around a core of categorical sensitivity—fulfilling the two most important criteria for a successful technology.

Most likely, all your life you've wondered what it is you would have to do to have people understand and agree with your way of doing things. Because of the very nature of behavior, the vast majority of us have long since abandoned the hope of finding this common denominator. The purpose of this book is the discovery of that miracle; that it truly exists and that it's yours for the asking. One must only use a modicum of effort to learn its secrets and become proficient in its use.

Interestingly, the very part of our lives where rapport should be most abundant is the very area where it's often the most lacking. As far as we've come technologically, and with as much progress as we've made, our relationships still remain one of the most rapport-starved corners of our lives. At the dawn of the 1990s, social scientists are still wondering how people will continue the frantic race to relate. It is my contention that to relate we must disengage our limiting two-dimensional model of relationships and begin a new process of relating, one in which we can continually expand and become truly relatable. I think that acquiring the skills of rapport is most crucial in the development of this process.

The ability to be in rapport with others is truly what

all of us want. With rapport technology, we're able to bypass persona, awkwardness, presentation, and rigidity by accessing the precise notes in another's scale of rapport. It's the ability to go right to the heart of empathy and place ourselves directly on the same wavelength. This process is not only interesting and enlightening but nourishing and nurturing to the parties involved.

As you acquire the skills of rapport technology, rapidly incorporating it as part of your behavioral resources, it will become obvious to you that it's applicable not only to personal relationships but to business relationships. In fact, for the most part, being successful in the business world is a direct function of rapport. It doesn't matter how terrific a product you make, or service you offer, if you fail at enrolling customers in yourself and, hence, in your company. Think about it. You are the living representation of your company. How often did you buy, or continue to buy, goods and services from someone with whom you were not in rapport, at least on some level? As a consumer, how often have you turned away from a product because you didn't feel good about the person from whom you were buying? As a businessman, how many deals have you lost through the unavailability of rapport? We've all had the experience of wanting—even needing—a product or service, yet avoiding its purchase, or seeking supply at another concern, simply because we didn't like the individual representing the company. Deals involving millions of dollars are predicated on rapport. Interesting, isn't it?—this need to like people or feel related to and understood by those we buy from. You'd think companies would understand this and train their representatives appropriately. But oftentimes this just isn't the case. After spending tens of millions of dollars on development, marketing, and advertising, these very same companies entrust the selling of their carefully created product to individuals who haven't the slightest notion of what rapport is, let alone how to produce it. The point is that in business, as in life, where there is no rapport there is no sale. Enrolling people in your product or service is the same as enrolling them in you. That's just the way it is.

As you learn more about rapport, you'll begin to notice where rapport is for you and how much of it you already have in your life. You'll probably find, as I did, that rapport is that "thing" you've been trying to have with people for as long as you remember. It was always in the air between you and others, just out of reach for want of a means of expression. It is through expression that rapport manifests itself among people, gently opening the space for relationships. If you look back over the successes you've had, almost always, the condition of rapport was present. What sometimes makes this hard to see is that rapport, like a catalyst in a chemical reaction, doesn't get involved in the mechanics of relating itself. It simply makes relating possible; or, more accurately, it creates the probability of a relationship. Ultimately, what one realizes is that without rapport, relationships and results are pretty hard to come by; with rapport, the result *is* the creation of relationships.

PART I

The Representational Types

1

RAPPORT DEFINED

OW that we know that rapport is an essential not only in our relationships but in life itself, how do we go about getting this elusive quality? Happily, rapport is a state that can be acquired rather quickly. You don't need a doctorate in philosophy to become sophisticated at establishing rapport. What you do need is commitment, determination, and a genuine desire to learn the skills involved in being a good rapport establisher. Interestingly, you've always had the ability to come to rapport with those around you, and have in fact unknowingly used that ability when you were so inclined. Much like Dorothy's ruby slippers and their ability to take her home, rapport is something that's been with you always—you just need to rediscover your access to it. I promise you it's there.

But just in case you doubt me, think back to a time when you and another person were really in harmony. It doesn't matter who this other person was. Go back and recall this time. What was it like? Maybe you shared a common experience of a group of people at a party, or a movie you watched together, or a Broadway show you both saw. If you think back, you'll see that what was happening between you and your friend was a mutual understanding of each other's map of the territory. You felt the same way about something because in many ways you are like each other. Your body language is probably similar, right down to your breathing patterns. Most likely, you and your pal move the same way, especially under certain circumstances. And, as you will learn, your speech patterns and eye movements are probably pretty much the same. In more than a few ways, that other person is probably like you. People fall into rapport very quickly and automatically with people who are like them. Think about it. Aren't you attracted to people who are like you or whom you want to be like? I mean, when you're with someone *opposite* from you, do you feel an urgency to make them a fast friend? Not really.

Rapport reverses a strict law of physics:
Instead of opposites attracting,
like *attracts* like.

When you're at a party and someone is being distasteful and obnoxious, do you want to run up and shoot the breeze with them, maybe share with them how things are running in your life? Of course not. You wouldn't think of doing that. Yet, some of us are in relationships—all kinds of relationships—that work exactly that way. We're with people we once upon a time found satisfaction with, but have since lost that fulfillment and have been unable to re-create it. We are out of rapport. We're stuck: caught in a dynamic short circuit that bounces us between our feelings of emotional warmth and logical doubt. What to do? Ah, there's the rub.

> ## People Like People Who Are Like Themselves

While it's great to have some spice in our rapport with others, people whose perception of the world is totally opposite ours, who look at things in a diametrically different way, are clearly harder for us to relate to. Now this may seem obvious to you at first, but step back and take a look at the relationships around you—maybe even your own— and you'll notice that people stay friends with, tend to love more honestly, and get along better with people who are like themselves. Specifically, if your model or map of the world is primarily a visual one—you see things as pictures and colors and lines and shapes—and you're relating with an auditory individual—someone who hears the world through words and tones and sounds—you'd better know how to navigate on *his* terrain. Because if you don't, your understanding of each other will be pretty much nonexistent. Struggling to find your way with an unfamiliar map of the territory is an exercise in utter futility. But if you know how to transpose yourself, to enter your friend's world of perceptual experience, you will be stunned at how easy it is to relate.

Because of the way we're put together, we gravitate to people who like the things we like and behave the way we do. Oh, I know there are times we're attracted to others who are very much opposite from us. And I know there's a myth flying around somewhere that opposites attract. But let me tell you this: when the initial challenge of opposite attraction wears off, we're left with someone who thinks, acts, and behaves unlike what *we* consider the norm. And consequently, that means someone who, for the most part, will be out of sync or out of rapport with us most of the time. Look no further for the cause of broken relationships. If you go back over the relationships of your life with an open mind and a not-so-microscopic eye, you'll almost always discover that their demise was the result of a rapportless foundation.

If you are involved with someone and a good part of the time you don't understand each other, you are out of rapport. And if you are out of rapport, the chances of your relationship surviving are slim to none. In fact, the duration of your relationship may be a testament to your persistence; for persistence and grim intention are what it takes to stay with another self when rapport is not present. It's a drag. Now, if you've happened to fall in love with this person with whom you have no rapport, what you have on your hands is a no-win situation, destined for failure.

Does that mean that the only people we can have serious relationships with or communicate well with are those who are just like us? Naturally not. It just means that if we want to love people who see things differently from us, or if we want to sell ourselves or our ideas to those whose maps of the territory are not in alignment with ours, we'll have to do something we've never consciously done before. That is, create rapport with them by being like them. People have rapport with others because of the reflection of themselves they perceive. The same holds true for being in rapport with ourselves or with the world around us. Those in rapport with their environment can see their likenesses reflected in the seasons. And those in rapport with themselves manifest behavior consistent with their purpose. Now this isn't some la-de-da belief that I'm asking you to swallow. It's a fact. Neurologically, we respond more congruently to similarity than to disparity. When we "fit" well with someone, we're more at ease than with someone who's incongruent with us. We must relearn our communication strategies so that we relate to others in a manner that fits their map of the world. That's what rapport is all about.

Being in rapport is the ability to enter someone else's model of the world and let them know that we truly understand their model.

AND

It's letting someone come into our frame of the world and having an experience of them truly understanding us.

The truth of it is, the only solution to rapportless relationships is the creation of rapport. Without it, the commonality, that "mutualness" of two together, is profoundly incomplete. Rapport is the foundation of successful and unencumbered communication. Hence, it's the bottom line in any relationship that has true value.

Rapport is essential to being an understanding and empathetic mate; an exciting and satisfying lover; a dynamic salesperson; an inspired leader; a nurturing parent. Without rapport, what's left are only our points of view—with all the right and wrong, blame and shame, fault and guilt attached to them.

Can you recall a time—maybe it was your birthday or anniversary or Christmas—when someone you cared for gave you a present? Can you remember opening it in their presence and seeing something you really disliked or that you felt wasn't you, or maybe it wasn't what you were really hoping for? How did you feel? What did you say? Probably, you put on the best smile you could muster and said something like: "Gosh, this is terrific, really terrific."

Now, can you also remember the expression on the other person's face? Chances are he knew—*really* knew—you didn't mean what you said. Maybe you thought you had fooled him, but somewhere in your mind you had a strong feeling you weren't getting away with anything. This is an illustration of *incongruency*. When your physiology, tone of voice, and words are incongruent—that is, not in alignment with one another—it is most difficult to effect rapport.

Now look at the other side of the coin. Remember when you held someone you cared for very close, looked at her in the softness of her eyes, and told her, "I love you"? Or when you explained to a friend how you were going to accomplish a much-wanted outcome? How about when you were bursting with pride at the promotion you got? These are examples of *congruency*. The image you had in your mind was in harmony with the way you expressed the thought. In the first example, the picture or visual image in your mind was *opposite* or incongruent with your physical demonstration. Congruency is an important axiom of rapport-technology. When we're congruent in our behavior—that is, when we're in agreement visually, auditorily, and kinesthetically—the result, with respect to our relationships, is rapport.

Being congruent with our eyes, ears, and feelings is largely dependent on how we internally represent experience. In our experience of life, we depend totally on our five senses to give us a composite picture of reality. We just don't have any other way of evaluating what's out there other than these five sensory channels. They are the source of our reality. So our experience, if you will, is a combination of what our eyes see; what our ears hear; what our touch feels *and* how we feel internally; and, to a lesser extent, what our tongue tastes and what our nose smells. Blended together, they create a frame of reality that belongs to us alone; no one really experiences it the same way we do. It is uniquely ours. We all, then, have our own reality, wonderful and distinct unto ourselves.

As we grow from infant to child to adult, we continue to integrate our experiences through our senses. But as time passes, one of these senses usually becomes dominant. In other words, we lean on that particular sense for representing much—but not all—of our experience. By *representing*, I mean the way in which we code what's out there in the world to how we perceive it. We also use this *"primary representational system"* to perform everyday behaviors and activities. I want to stress that we never stop using our other sensory modalities. It's simply that we gradually begin to have a preference with respect to representing experience primarily through that particular highly valued sensory channel. So if we represent experience for the most part visually, through pictures and images, we could say that we're primarily visual. If we make sense of our surroundings largely through the sense of sound, we'd call ourselves auditories. Likewise, if feeling or touching supplies us with most of our worldly perceptions, we'd term ourselves kinesthetics, from the Latin *kinesthesia*. For our purposes, and to simplify our study, taste and smell will not be discussed. In statistical comparison, they account for a very small percentage of primary or leading representational systems. And, lest you think that auditories have better hearing, or visuals better eyesight—or even that kinesthetics have a better sense of feeling—let me be clear that this isn't the case. Being auditory, for example, simply means that you depend on your ears more than, say, your eyes. And this is a good point. Lots of people have behaviors that make use of a less efficient representational system for a particular behavior. For instance, athletes are usually kinesthetic—they depend on touch. If, however, you want to be a terrific football defensive end, and you're an auditory, you might have a problem. Hearing strategies in sports are *not* highly valued, for the most part. However, being auditory *is* a highly prized strategy for musicians or cardiologists. Similarly, the best strategy for the simple task of spelling is visual. When we can visualize a word, it makes it a thousand times easier to spell properly. However, most of us have learned to spell by auditory discrimination, which is a uniformly terrible way to construct words. Remember being told in school to "sound out" words to figure out how to spell them? For a word that sounds the way it is spelled, such as "fun," this is fine. But in a word like "taught," there are three letters that do not have an individual sound. The only way to learn these words correctly is to use a visual strategy—chunk the words into visually remembered sections and see them in your mind. So we have a nation full of lousy spellers because somewhere in the beginning the person who originally taught spelling was auditory.

Our three main sensory channels, then, supply us with the sum total of our experience. I call them "representational systems," as they represent reality as we experience it.

    I. Representational Systems
       1. Visual = pictures, images
       2. Auditory = sounds, tones
       3. Kinesthetic = touch, feelings

    II. *Primary* Representational System
      The particular representational system
      we individually tend to favor.

There is a direct correlation between our representational type and our biochemical and physiological states. At first this might be difficult to accept, but think about it a moment. Someone who experiences the world primarily through pictures is going to be different physically from someone who interprets the world through feelings or sounds. We will discuss the implications of this as we learn more about the technology of rapport in part II, but for now what concerns us is *how* this works, and how it is manifest in the body. Let's look at some of the ways this is so.

The Physiology of Rapport

    I. The first and most important physical characteristic of representational type is the eye accessing cue. Quite simply, when one accesses either pictures, words, or feelings, one uses the eyes to stimulate the corresponding areas of the brain. It's an involuntary action, one that we do thousands of times each day. This is a scientifically observed result of psychological studies. It's a theory of neurobiology, for instance, that when people move their eyes up and to the left, their neural pathways stimulate remembered (eidetic) images found in the nondominant right hemisphere of the cerebral cortex. These neural pathways, located on the left sides of both eyes, are represented in the corresponding visual part of the brain, and help us to access visual memory. There are specific cues for accessing the other representational systems as well. The eye accessing cue may be thought of as a catalyst in a chemical equation. The catalyst doesn't partake in the reaction, it simply stimulates the reaction to occur without getting involved itself. We'll learn more about the specifics of eye accessing technology in chapter 7, but for now all we need to know is that visuals, auditories, and kinesthetics each have different eye patterns for accessing information.

II. Our breathing pattern—the style, if you will, of our respiration—is linked with our state of mind. Recall a time when you observed friends in a state of excitement. You'll clearly remember how different their breathing patterns were as compared to when they were functioning normally. Breathing patterns will be affected differently by internally and externally generated pictures, sounds, and feelings. These patterns of inhalation and exhalation have a direct correlation with our biochemical and physiological states. The rate at which we breathe and the location of breath in the lung cavity directly affect different muscle groups and literally change the chemical composition of our blood. Since our brain is fully saturated with blood at all times, and our blood chemistry is affected by our breathing style, it follows that our pattern of breathing affects our consciousness and thus our conscious states. In other words, by affecting blood chemistry, our breathing style changes our neurology and consequently our attitudinal state. Changes in breathing styles and patterns are a very good indicator of representational system cues, and this is another way we determine which system predominates in a person, and which system they may be accessing at any given time.

III. As the breathing patterns change, they directly influence vocal tempo, intonation, and pitch. These changes are caused by variances in muscle tension in the face and neck area. The quantity and tidal volume of air being blown over the visual's vocal cords, for example, will influence this person's vocal style.

IV. There is also a correlation between a person's body type and his primary representational system. This body style is the result of our continuing use of certain strategies or behavioral traits over a long period of time. Naturally, muscle tension, metabolism, and biophysics also contribute to the formation of the primary representational system one acquires.

I have divided this book into two main sections. The first examines in depth the three main representational systems, starting with the Rapport Representational Strategic Inventory, a short, simple quiz to help you determine your representational type. I recommend that you take the quiz first, before proceeding to learn about each particular type. It will help you understand how you approach life and why you do some things better than others.

In part II, the technology of rapport establishment is explained. Starting with the most basic, each technology is discussed and demonstrated, layer upon layer, until by chapter 10 you will learn how to make all the technologies work together to create deep rapport in any situation. For this reason, it's best to read these chapters in order.

That rapport is the foundation for all successful relationships and unfettered communication is obvious. It is the very cornerstone of human relations. We are creatures of rapport, or the absence of it, depending on it to make our communication work. When we are knowledgeable about an undertaken project, we have confidence in our competence. If we have a sense of certainty about our competence, we might even feel good about the project. Yet, if we're in rapport with the others involved, we have a recipe for success. You see, in many ways, rapport is a residue of design. It is the glue that holds competence and certainty together. Leadership, excellence, and full self-expression are the result of relationships rich with high rapport.

2

THE RAPPORT REPRESENTATIONAL STRATEGIC INVENTORY

T HE following test is designed to discover your primary representational system and the first representational component in many of your strategies. By knowing this, you'll be able to see how you lead with other representational systems besides your primary one.

Answer each question with the very first response that comes to mind. If you have trouble deciding between two answers, check the one that occurs to you first. There is no need for undue thought and pondering as though your life depended on how you answer. That's a waste of time. Your first response is usually the most appropriate. If you're still having a difficult time choosing, think of specific circumstances in your life—relative to the question—that come closest to approximating the answer. If all else fails, simply pick one of the possible choices. Most likely that will be the most appropriate one. If you get a sudden case of the "how I might make the test come out the way I want to" syndrome, try to resist. Purposely slanting your responses will make the outcome meaningless and will rip you off of information from which you could benefit.

There is no representational system that is better or worse than the others. Everywhere in life you'll find people who are lords or serfs, rich or poor, enlightened or foolhardy, connected or disenfranchised, gentle or bellicose, who represent experience visually, auditorily, and kinesthetically. Life doesn't divide the good into one sensory channel and the bad into others. Your representational type doesn't have any relevance to what kind of human being you are; it simply sheds light on how you relate *as* a human being. And reveals how you run your relationships.

1. **When you recall a time you were immensely drawn to someone, what was the very *first* thing that attracted you to them? Was it:**

a. The way they looked.
b. Something they said to you, or that you heard.
c. The way they touched you, or something you felt.

2. **When you recall a particularly wonderful vacation you had, what's the very *first* experience you remember? Was it:**

a. The way the resort area looked.
b. The different way it sounded to you.
c. The feeling you got by vacationing there.

3. **When you drive, how do you navigate?**

a. I look for road signs or follow a map of the territory.
b. I listen for familiar sounds that point me in the right direction.
c. I get a gut feeling or sense of where I am.

4. **When I engage in my favorite sport, I particularly enjoy:**

a. The look of the game, or how I look playing it.

b. The sound of the game, such as the thwack of the ball or the roar of the crowd.

c. The feel of the game, such as the grip of the club or the sense of motion.

5. When I get an assignment at work, it is easier to understand and to execute if:

a. It's written or diagrammed.

b. It's explained to me.

c. I get a sense of clarity, purpose, or correctness from it.

6. When my problems get me down, I find it helps to:

a. Write them down so I can see them clearly.

b. Talk or listen to another until my problems sound easier to hear.

c. Sort them out internally until they make sense.

7. I find it easier to be with my friends if:

a. They communicate using animation and to-the-point statements.

b. They interact with me through easy-to-hear and varying speech.

c. I get a feeling that they know where I'm coming from.

8. When I make decisions, it helps to:

a. Picture the possible choices in my mind's eye.

b. Hear both sides of a dialogue within my mind.

c. Sense how I would feel if either choice came to pass.

9. Which group do I tend to favor:

a. Photography, painting, reading, sketching, films.

b. Music, musical instruments, the sound of the sea, wind chimes, concerts.

c. Ball games, woodworking, massage, introspection, touching.

10. During sex, I like to:

a. Look at what's going on.

b. Hear my lover.

c. Feel every sensation.

11. When I buy an article of clothing, after first seeing it, the *very next* thing I do is:

a. Take another really good look at it or picture myself wearing it.

b. Listen closely to the salesperson and/or have a conversation with myself giving the pros and cons of buying it.

c. Get a feeling about it and/or touch it to see if it's something I'd enjoy wearing.

12. On the occasions when I think of a former lover, the *very first* thing I do is:

a. See the person in my mind's eye.

b. Hear his or her voice in my mind.

c. Get a certain feeling about the person.

13. At the gym, my experience of satisfaction comes *first* from:

a. Seeing myself in the mirror getting better.

b. Hearing myself or others say how good I'm looking.

c. Feeling my body get stronger and sensing it's more in shape.

14. When I have occasion to use mathematics, I verify my answer by:

a. Looking at the numbers to see if they look correct.
b. Counting the numbers in my head.
c. Using my fingers to get a sense of correctness.

15. When I spell, I verify accuracy by:

a. Looking at the word in my mind's eye to see if it looks the way that word should.
b. Saying the word out loud or hearing it in my mind.
c. Getting a feeling about the way the word is spelled.

16. The subject I enjoyed the most in school came about *primarily* as a result of:

a. The way it looked on the board or in books.
b. The sound of the subject as it was taught to me.
c. My sense of interest as I learned more about it.

17. When I love someone, I get an immediate experience of:

a. The way we look together through the eyes of love.
b. The sound of telling him or her or being told, "I love you."
c. A feeling or sense of warmth toward that person.

18. When I turn off to someone, I get an immediate experience of dislike:

a. When I see them approach.
b. When they begin talking to me.
c. When I sense they're nearby.

19. At the beach, the very first thing that makes me glad to be there is:

a. The look of the sand, the smiling sun, and the ice-blue water.

b. The sound of the waves, the laughing wind, and distant whispers.

c. The feel of the sand, the salt air on my lips, and the joy of serenity.

20. Having a conversation at a party, my whole frame of experience will change if:

a. The lights get brighter or dimmer.

b. The music changes pace.

c. The room temperature changes.

21. I know my career is taking a turn for the better when:

a. I see myself moving into the corner office.

b. I hear the chief executive say, "You're really going to go places."

c. I feel satisfaction in getting a promotion.

22. Before going to sleep at night, it's important that:

a. The room is nearly dark or pleasantly shaded.

b. The room is hushed or muted with pleasing background quiet.

c. The bed feels very comfortable.

23. In the morning, I especially enjoy awakening to:

a. Either the sun streaming in or an overcast day.

b. The sound of a lively wind or rain pelting the windows.

c. A warm and toasty comforter or flannel sheets.

24. When I experience anxiety, the very first thing that happens is:

a. The world takes on a different appearance in some way.

b. Sounds begin to bother me.

c. My sense of ease begins to alter.

25. When I'm very happy, my world:

a. Takes on a definite and wonderful shine.

b. Resonates with total harmony.

c. Fits perfectly within the space of my life.

26. I get along better with people who:

a. Relate to the world through the way it looks.

b. Relate to the world through the way it sounds.

c. Relate to the world through the way it makes them feel.

27. When I get totally motivated, the *first* thing that happens is:

a. I see things from a new and resourceful perspective.

b. I tell myself how this state is going to create new possibilities.

c. I can actually feel myself getting psyched up.

28. When someone tells me, "I love you," my *first* experience is:

a. An image of the person loving me, or us together.

b. A dialogue within my soul saying, "This is wonderful."

c. A feeling of pleasurable contentment.

29. Death, for me, is probably:

a. To see no more, or to see in a totally new way.

b. To hear no more, or to hear in a totally new way.

c. To feel no more, or to feel in a totally new way.

30. Having rapport with someone is:

a. Seeing him or her in a wonderful and easy-to-be-with way.

b. Hearing the person communicate things exactly the way I would.

c. Feeling toward the person the way I know he or she feels toward me.

Now, add up the three separate scores of A's, B's, and C's. The letter with the highest number indicates that this is probably your primary representational system.

$$A's = Visual$$
$$B's = Auditory$$
$$C's = Kinesthetic$$

If you score a 10 in each category, take the test over in a day or so; you'll probably find one area predominates. If your three scores are still close together in value, it means that though you might be primarily visual, for example, many of your strategies are kinesthetic or auditory. If your scores are highly skewed, that is to say, higher than 17 in any category, you are clearly dominant in that representational system.

3

THE VISUAL REPRESENTATIONAL TYPE

T is through the visual's perspective—the eyes of the true connoisseur—that most of our planet's beauty shines through. They are the interpreters of the geometry of our world and are also its graphic artists and color coordinators. Somewhere along the way, these people's visual systems became not only much more developed but actually the primary way in which they experience the world.

Fully 60 percent of the population is visual. There is no clear explanation of why this is so. Perhaps, for the majority of us, we were taught from birth to depend on our eyes, our sense of sight, in order to make our way in the world. Or maybe it's because eyesight is such a dominant sense that we instinctively use vision more than any other modality. Or it could be that our society, indeed the world we live in, is primarily programmed by visual cues. Our zeitgeist is the information society. Our input is through television and movies and hard copy. What den doesn't have the green fog of a computer terminal beaming through its nighttime window? Visuality is the dominant representational system of our time.

Visual people are movers and shakers. They are constantly traveling at speeds approaching that of light. Sometimes they exceed even that speed and transform themselves into pure energy. Since they are creatures of the light and are extremely mobile, it's easy to find them in professions that allow them visual expression. Nowhere is this more easily observable than in the entertainment industry. Here we can easily see visuals really being visual, with their characteristic physical style of swift movement. Visuals are drawn to this industry and its related fields as a natural expression of who they are. You'll also see visuals, quite obviously, in the visual arts such as painting, photography, and design. They also make great marksmen, firefighters, and pilots.

Following is a small list of some famous visual people. Can you picture in your mind the qualities that make them visual dominants?

> Clark Gable
> Bruce Willis
> Lily Tomlin
> Roger Moore
> David Letterman
> Robin Williams

Can you see some of the common characteristics visuals share? David Letterman's speech patterns are remarkably akin to Lily Tomlin's. Both use lots of visual description when communicating. Tomlin's alter egos are created strictly out of visual imagery. And how good an interviewer would Letterman be if we couldn't watch his facial grimaces as he responds to his guests' statements? Bruce Willis's popularity is based almost totally on his ability to make us feel a particular way about him through his appearance. Clark Gable had the same appeal. His acting depended not so much on what he said but on how we reacted to the look of his characters. Roger Moore is another example of visual acting. If you took away his facial contortions, you'd be removing 90 percent of his artistic prowess. And need I really explain Robin Williams? Try closing your eyes and enjoying him in concert. Pretty much an impossibility—that's how visual he is. Yet look at the richness these people give us. To every representation, there comes an intrinsic opportunity for genius. That's the miracle of communication through rapport.

Though it's relatively easy to categorize the obviously visual, it's important to remember that the other representational systems, audition and kinesthesia, have quite an influence even on the most visual people we know. No one is dedicated exclusively to any one system. Even the most extreme visuals will use their other senses to perform specific tasks or strategies in the process of living. One of my good friends is a true visual, yet he depends on an auditory strategy of internal dialogue when he reads. Though clearly visually dominant, he must also hear the words to make sense of what he sees. Similarly, Albert Einstein, a kinesthetic, used a singular visual strategy—visualizing pictures of polynomial expressions—to navigate around the world of numbers he had to deal with every day. In fact, the most famous representation of his theory, $E = mc^2$, which depicts a man actually riding on a beam of light, is totally visual. And though John Fitzgerald Kennedy was auditory, his strategy for manifesting authority was starkly visual. This first came across to the American people in the televised debates between Kennedy and Nixon. It is now universally agreed that Kennedy won those debates, but at the time, those listening on radio—who had no access to the visual style of Kennedy—felt Nixon had won. Kennedy's impression was created solely through visual representation. (Since that time, visual characterizations have played an ever-increasing role in political campaigns.) Later, when Kennedy was president, he used those skills again and again, most impressively during the Cuban Missile Crisis. When he appeared on television he looked the part of a leader, and he looked like he meant what he said. Even the Russians could see that.

All of us share some visual qualities. Indeed, it would be an unfortunate soul who didn't have access to his visual representational system. Although I'm about as auditory as one can get, I'd be lost without my visual strategy for explanation. Ever since I can remember, people have told me, almost without fail, how wonderful it was to listen to me describe a scene from a movie or a book, or the way I could give them a picture of something they had never seen for themselves. When I remember something from my past, in my mind I see it as though it were a lifelike photograph projected onto a screen. And, true to visual strategy, as soon as those pictures come to life and give me what I want, they fade and run, like a warm palette of colors. But because I lead with my auditory representational system, these pictures usually flow with a narration of the image or a dialogue on the meaning of that image. And how well I hear it depends on the picture's emotional impact. That differentiates me from leading either visually or kinesthetically.

Visual people, as I've said, also have auditory and kinesthetic representational systems wired in from birth. And even the most extreme visual will have auditory and kinesthetic strategies for certain behaviors. A client of mine who is a paint and color coordinator for Mercedes-Benz and is highly visual has an attraction strategy that is almost totally kinesthetic. When she meets someone to whom she's instantly drawn, her attraction is based on a "feeling" she gets during those first few minutes. In fact, the way a man looks holds the least priority in her attraction strategy. This doesn't mean she's less visual, only that her strategy for being attracted to someone begins with a kinesthetic first step. This is invaluable both for her and others to know, as it will influence her relationships all her life.

Rather than complicating our knowledge of visuals, an understanding of their system traits sheds light on the impact they have on us. And they do have impact. First, they comprise a large number of people in the world, so we know that our lives will bear their influence. Second, since sight is such a strong perceptual system shared by many people, in many cultures, very often the world is mapped out by those who are visually oriented. Auditories and kinesthetics must learn to accommodate to these standards or fall by the wayside. In a sense they would lead rapportless lives. And herein lies a fundamental problem. How do auditories and kinesthetics establish high enough rapport that they not only transcend the communication barrier with visuals, but enrich themselves as a result of establishing rapport? The first step in answering this question is to take an in-depth look at the visual. Who is this person? What does he look like? How does she think? And, how do we find rapport with these people?

Physical Manifestations and Body Types of the Visual

Breathing Style

If you notice that someone's respiration tends to be high in the chest and is often shallow, that person is probably visual. When you ask a visual a question that stimulates his pictures, such as, "Where do you spend your summers?" or, "How would you teach me to ski?" you will notice that he momentarily stops breathing while accessing the picture required to answer your question. Visuals *see* themselves in the pictures of their answers. As a new picture forms, their breathing begins again. As you become a better and more fluent rapport builder, you'll even notice that visuals lose a little color in their faces as they access their images. And when they complete their scanning, their color returns. They flush. This is a sure sign that someone is in the visual mode.

Voice

The visual personality has an expressive voice. It's usually enthusiastic. They speak in a somewhat staccato fashion and sometimes in quick bursts. Their voices tend to be high pitched and might have a strained tonal quality.

Musculature

Visuals tend to be slightly on the ectomorphic side. This means that often, but certainly not always, they are lanky, with long waists and thin bodies. However, there are definite exceptions to the rule. Heavyset visuals are everywhere, and are sometimes referred to as "thin people in heavy bodies."

When visuals access pictures, their bodies tend to tense up. Sometimes this is obvious, as when they rub their necks while thinking about something. Visuals also tighten their abdominal muscles and tense their shoulders while reaching into their thoughts for an image.

When being expressive, visuals often point to their eyes or out in front of themselves, as if an imaginary easel exists there. They use these gestural accessing cues as a means to stimulate or access their thoughts, and it is an indication that they are in the visual mode. It's not unusual to hear a visual say, "I don't understand you," while pointing to his eyes.

Eye Accessing Cues

The visual will look up frequently, to the right or left, and stay in that position while accessing a thought longer than other types.

Though visuals comprise the majority, in some ways they are the least understood. Because of their vitality, they are often mistaken as arrogant. With a thought process that speeds along at warp 1, their level of patience with others is not what you would call overwhelming. And their emotional life is... well, it's not often laced with undue sensitivity. Because they relate to the world through images and pictures, both from the past and the future, visuals are more deft than others at letting go of their emotions. That's not to say they're cold or intolerant; they're just not mired in the vicissitudes of emotional swings. You won't often see a visual emotionally distraught for a prolonged period of time over a love affair that's gone awry. They create pictures so quickly that it's possible for them to escape the tempest of highs and lows that frequently accompany ragged relationships. Now you can imagine how unsuitable this strategy makes them for someone who values sensitivity and feelings very highly, such as a kinesthetic! Yet, all around us we see visuals in working and viable relationships with kinesthetics and auditories. These visuals, whether they are conscious of it or not, have mastered the ability of rapport. Their relationships work. But what about those of us who are trying to get to know or understand or communicate with a visual? How do we attempt this? Let's take a look at three scenarios that typify the common, rapportless way in which people make an effort at being understood.

You're auditory. Your boss is visual. You come to work prepared to tell her how you've accomplished some great task, and you don't understand why she can't hear what you're saying. You rethink what you've said, adding some more pertinent information to the dialogue, and still she looks at you as though you're speaking Mandarin. As you leave her office, you swear she's from a different galaxy and chalk off the meeting as "one of those things." Except it isn't. First, she really doesn't "hear" what you're saying; second, you'd better find a way to get her to understand you if you want to stay employed.

Your boyfriend is visual. It's Saturday and you've decided to really make his day. You make sure the house has a fresh scent to it, that it creates a feeling of closeness and togetherness. You fill the bedroom with music that makes you feel sensual and attractive, and when he comes back from his weekly softball game, you tell him how much you've missed him, that he fills up your senses like a night in the forest, and you ask how he feels about going to the George Winston concert under the stars tonight. His reply to all this is a really wide yawn followed by an impromptu nap. When you react to this by getting upset, he simply says he doesn't see what's bothering you.

You're kinesthetic. You walk into the black-tie party your company has thrown for its junior partners and you're feeling great. You got the Weintraub deal, the boss is impressed, life works. Across the crowded room you notice her gazing at you with an enchanted smile. The music plays, the dancers glide, you pad across the boards to end up standing shoulder to shoulder with her. A friend introduces you. You tell her how exciting it is to be a part of all this, that you sense she really feels wonderful about being here tonight, and how pleased you'd be if she would accept the next dance. She looks at you painfully and says sincerely, "I don't see what you mean." You crumble.

We've all had these experiences. They are frustrating—even demoralizing. But what went wrong in each case? Clearly, rapport was noticeably absent. We can achieve rapport by utilizing the technology for its development. And one of the first clues we have to what representational group someone belongs to, and hence what guide we should follow to initiate rapport, is easily found just by observing language.

Language

Though all of us are a mix of the visual, auditory, and kinesthetic representational systems, we tend to use "processing" words that are in alignment with either our primary representational system or the representational system we're leading with at the moment. As an example, the visual person will express his understanding of you by saying:

That's **clear** to me.

I **see** what you mean.

That's a horse of a different **color.**

Can you **picture** that?

I want to get a better **perspective.**

Let's **focus** in on this.

Now I see the **light.**

The degree to which *linguistic representation* correlates is quite high. We tend to use language that is intimately bonded with our thoughts. In other words, if we are primarily visual, we'll represent that by talking "visually." We'll use visual words. Those words highlighted above are examples of these representational "processors." And they not only shed light on who is visual but give us a place to begin our journey into their world.

In the three previous dramas, we saw pretty clearly how *not* to be in rapport from the get-go. In all three cases, the parties involved missed the mark by talking in opposing systems. I mean that it should start to dawn on you by now that answering the question: "Do you **see** anything in the **long**

view that could **clearly** be a problem for us?" with: "No. My **sense** of it is that everything fits **nice** and **snug** and we should be home free..." is begging for trouble. I can't tell you how just this little incongruity will substantially reduce your chances of being in rapport. Conversely, offering back language in the *same representational system* is like completing the circuit on an electronic door opener. Really, without any energy at all, an answer such as: "Nope. I don't **see** anything that **looks** even one **shade** off, from my point of **view**," will immediately place you in the perfect trajectory for instant rapport. You see, by mirroring, or offering back, language that is in kind, in the same representational context as what's being communicated to us, we open the window of rapport.

In chapter 6, "The Language of Rapport," we'll learn incredible technologies for quickly establishing rapport with the simplicity of language alone.

If we composed a picture of a visual, what would we see? Would we recognize them at a business meeting or at a party? How about at the club or on the street? Well, by now we have a pretty good idea of what to look for. Still, let's see if we can condense what we've learned into one composite to serve as a general description of our visual.

Visuals have a medium build but could easily be lanky or even heavyset. They tend to use their arms and hands a lot when talking. They're breathy when communicating and respiration is high in the chest and often shallow. When they access pictures, they tend to tighten their abdomen and shoulder muscles.

They often speak in quick bursts of words and may have a strained tonality in their voices. In addition, their voices tend to be high-pitched when accessing images. Speech may have a fast tempo when they start to flip through these images.

Visual eye accessing cues are pretty obvious most of the

time—but not always. Usually visuals glance to the upper right or left, depending on whether they're looking at something in memory (upper left for right-handed people, upper right for left-handed people) or seeing something they haven't visualized before (upper right for right-handed people, upper left for left-handed people). Occasionally, though, they'll momentarily switch to the other system cues while attaching narration, dialogue, or feeling to the picture. (For more on eye accessing cues, see chapter 7.)

Sometimes they'll point to the eyes or eye area while pausing to "see" something. Rubbing the neck while pondering is also a common gestural cue.

Their verbal processing words can be highly visual. "That's **clear** to me," or, "I **see** what you mean," or, "When I **look** at it that way ..." are typical of the visual language they use.

Visuals must learn to temper their state of high mobility with sensitivity. Beware of those who see only their own points of view. In fact, point of view is what visuals are all about. Those visuals who *have* a point of view can go on to wonderful heights and truly become soldiers of aliveness. Those who *become* their point of view can murder life with clandestine and surreptitious strategies.

Visual lovers can be a whirlwind of fantasy and mobility. They assume that their partners can see how they feel. "I mean, isn't it obvious?" they will ask you. With a visual, feelings are a subject you will have to approach through the world of pictures, not the one of words. If you ask your visual if she loves you, it's important to remember that she'll end up with a picture of the answer, even if she attaches feelings or a dialogue to it. When you ask this kind of question, pay attention to the visual's breathing and state of physiology. It will supply visual information as to what pictures she's generating at the moment. If you ask, "How do you feel about us?" you'll notice that she first looks to the lower right to get the correct feeling response, then to the upper right to see a picture of herself and you together looking good, or a picture of herself and you together looking bad, or (oh no!) a picture of herself—alone!

Visuals are active lovers. And though incredibly imaginative, they may get carried away with how things look in bed rather than what's going on. Visual fantasies rate high on their list of sexual priorities, and they like to see what's happening. A darkened room literally cuts them off from their experience.

They'll see their love for you (or lack of it) as clear as a crystal. But typically, visuals are not overly emotional. Being in love is, for them, either an image of two people joined together, or a picture of themselves loving you. They like to touch, but don't depend on feeling to validate their experience. Visuals often carry photographs of their lovers wherever they travel, and, of course, they enjoy a good love story at the movies. Having a loving rapport with a visual places an importance and priority on demonstration rather than verbal communication.

Being in rapport with visuals requires patience and understanding of the way they interpret the world. If you love them very much, you'll soon come to realize, *the map is not the territory*. Vision is just a guidepost or map enabling us to enter their world of subjective experience. As complicated as they are, being in rapport with them can be light and breezy.

They love the sunrise but also appreciate a good rainstorm. They'll admire the look on your face as you laugh more than the sound of the laughter itself. Take them to an exciting play rather than the symphony. Excite them with fresh lines and shapes and combine dashes of color to dazzle their retinas. Vacation with them at the Grand Canyon, not a lazy tropical beach.

Work for the visual at your own peril. These individuals want you to be totally clear, concise, and unmercifully to-the-point—because they are. Flowing and flowery language means nary a thing to them, and if you don't find that out quickly, you may be in big trouble. Don't humor them—produce, and get the job done. If you want to give your visual boss a birthday present, make sure it's something he won't get tired of looking at. And please, don't assume that because they're visual everything must be bright. They're sensitive to flashy items and can be offended by overly bright or sparkly things.

This above all: *Let them be visual,* and give them the moments they need to see their pictures in focus. Establish rapport with them ASAP. You may not have a second chance.

4

THE AUDITORY REPRESENTATIONAL TYPE

Those ideas that please me I retain in memory and am accustomed as I have been told to hum them to myself. If I continue this way, it soon occurs to me how I may turn this or that morsel to good account...that is to say agreeably to the rules of counterpoint, to the peculiarities of the various instruments, etc. All this fires my soul and...my subject enlarges itself and...though it be long, stands almost complete and finished in my mind....Nor do I hear in my imagination the parts successively, but I hear them, as it were, all at once. What a delight this is, I cannot tell....What has been thus produced, I do not easily forget.

—Wolfgang Amadeus Mozart

Sounds can send auditory people into either pure ecstasy or total madness! They relate to the world through the way things sound and in many respects are more sensitive to this representational system than visual people are to sight. Auditory people can be easily distracted by the most inoffensive sound—even (and especially) the most pleasant sounds—and will often interrupt a conversation by saying, "I'm sorry, could you repeat that?" It's not that they aren't paying attention. In fact, it's precisely because their attention is so funneled into the production of sound that a stray noise or distant roll of thunder can distract them. They should not be confused, though, with inattentive listeners. In fact, you might say that cultivated auditories are listening perfection. Auditories are verbal communicators. They enjoy dialogue—with others as well as themselves. Because of their innate ability internally to put thoughts into dialogue, oftentimes at great length, it's my belief that auditories are the loners of our culture. Wrapped in a world where it's possible for them to narrate life itself, some auditories can be alone for long periods of time. This can make them at once both very independent and needy. Serenity can be a long time coming when auditories are cut off from others. But this is the exception, and for the most part auditories produce the loveliest sounds that life can offer.

Auditory individuals travel about their business with grace, and are usually eager to listen to another's story. More than visuals or kinesthetics, auditories have an incredible ability to listen so thoroughly and with such intent that sonic data is absorbed and processed in their minds without the necessity of being translated into pictures (as with visuals) or feelings (as with kinesthetics). Because of this enhanced ability, auditories tend to gravitate to areas in life that permit the use of such superb listening and communicative talents.

When we consider these people, it is, of course, easy to imagine them as perfectly pitched musicians, audio aficionados, linguists, and singers; not to mention record producers, psychotherapists, clergy, and orators. However, to classify these people of tone and sound with a limiting definition is wasteful and purposeless. For nowhere in the world can we find any individual who is comprised of only one representational system.

Auditories listen to the world and hear what the world is saying—what its creatures are trying to let them know. Auditories relate to their environment through sound, as though nature had a voice; and they're talented, feeling translators, able to put the essence of an emotional sense into a frame of poetry.

Auditories possess a wonderful sensitivity to animals and may truly consider themselves part of the brotherhood of creatures. If you have ever noticed someone kneeling and talking to his pet, you've most likely heard an auditory in action.

Because of their heightened sensitivity to sound, auditories don't tolerate harsh or disharmonic noise as well as others do. Fire or ambulance sirens are major offenders, and though it may look comical, you can spot an auditory easily by observing who on a street corner is holding his ears as a hook-and-ladder speeds by, horns wailing. It's not exactly the high volume that's intolerable, it's more contextual than that. It's sound without form or symmetry that will frazzle an auditory.

If you want to hang out with an auditory, or if you want to marry one or live with one, please, be kind to his ears. Moving to an apartment facing a busy metropolitan street would be like flashing a bright strobe light in the eyes of a visual. Better to face the courtyard, where the muffled hiss of steam will soothe. Better still, live in the country or as close to an open area as possible. If you really want to please an auditory, incorporate the mellow sounds of a brook or bubbling stream into his living space—but not too loudly. Subtlety is the password to his domain. Do this, and you are immeasurably increasing the chances of successful rapport.

Auditories are not quite as locomotive as visuals; they

are more judicious with their motion, even more deliberate. When they walk, they flow. Not suited for jerky motions, auditories make wonderful magicians and natural surgeons. Operating rooms filled with music have auditory anesthesiologists keeping the flow.

Auditories admire graceful attitudes and respond to smooth but nonmanipulative presentations. They will come to rapport with almost anyone who has elegant speech. This doesn't mean those around them must be great orators, just a little more conscious of how they're presenting information. If you want a surefire way to turn off an auditory, speak in a monotone. Their eyes will defocus, and somewhere inside their being they will shift to a more satisfying dialogue, oftentimes with themselves.

Auditory people who are not aware of their inclination to sounds may sometimes dominate a conversation. If anyone is capable of running off at the mouth, it is these people. "She chewed my ear off" is an expression that kinesthetic people will use in this regard. And visual people will refer to a talkative auditory as someone who "talked until I was blue in the face." Visuals run through their pictures so fast that what auditories consider richly textured dialogue, visuals judge as "off-center" or "not to the point." Kinesthetics may drown in a plethora of feeling states as an auditory friend rolls along at a brisk clip of exact points. If you interrupt a rambling auditory middiscourse, he will tend to shut off the dialogue and be all ears to what you are about to say. Admittedly, though, some educated, erudite auditories are brutal conversation monopolizers, and establishing rapport with them can be most challenging.

Though auditories are likable sorts, and are easily identifiable, it's important to keep in mind that they also make use of the other representational systems to perform everyday behaviors. There is no such thing as an absolute auditory. Although you will doubtless run into someone who you'll swear "comes totally from sound," I urge you to refrain from evaluating all of her behavior as though she operated from that one system alone. As I've said, for a particular behavior or task, we sometimes lead with a different representational system, or sense, than our primary system. This means that an auditory might use a highly developed sense of sight when discriminating what attracts her to a mate. You would say that her "strategy" for attraction is visual. Another auditory might use his nimble sense of feeling for selling his company's computers. His strategy for selling is kinesthetic. What binds these two together is their auditory *primary* representational system: the one they use for the majority of tasks they perform. Let me give you an example. Though I am definitely an auditory, my strategy for navigation—for finding my way around the mountainous areas of where I live—is strictly kinesthetic! After spending time in a new part of the forest, I find my way home *primarily* by the feeling I get about my surroundings. Further, though I immensely enjoy the company of other auditories and form an instant rapport with them, when I speak to groups, I tend to paint visual images. So my strategy for communication to large groups is visual. Yet, I'm definitely auditory and I respond largely to things I can hear. More than anything else, the way something sounds is what does it for me. When I get excited, thrilled, charged—even inspired—it's usually through some sort of internal or external auditory stimulation. That's what gets my bells to ring.

When we take a qualitative and comparative look at auditories, it becomes evident that these people of sound must coexist in a world sometimes hostile to their innate style of relating. The world, for the most part, is not a quiet, hushed, harmonious place, and everywhere life will be a challenge to the auditory. Being somewhat under 20 percent of the population, statistically they are surrounded by people who relate to them through vision and sensation. In other words, the auditory exists in a world where the rules for most behaviors have been written largely by visuals, and, to a lesser degree, by kinesthetics. It's obvious, then, that an auditory should have not only a keen understanding of the other two primary systems and how they manifest themselves, but a strong sense of self-knowing. Consistent with this class of behavior is the importance of natural relating... of rapport.

What must we do to establish complete, successful rapport with auditories? Can we do it and come away from the experience not only relating to them but somehow better off? For us to answer these questions, we need to take an in-depth look at auditories. Who are they, and how will you know them?

Physical Manifestations and Body Types of the Auditory

Breathing Style

Observing auditories while in conversation, you'll notice that they exhibit a rather regular and rhythmic flow of breath. Auditories tend to use all of the diaphragm or all of the chest, sometimes combining both in a rather fluid and mobile respiration. President Reagan does this almost all the time. Very often, when he's asked a question, he'll look to the lower left for the dialogue while smoothly inhaling and saying, "Well..." In fact, he often shakes his head slightly—as if arriving at the answer—just before actually coming out with his response.

It's fascinating to watch an auditory access her vast file of sounds and dialogue as a conversation progresses. Ask an auditory to recall her last vacation, and you'll be aware of the occurrence of a protracted exhalation—in effect, what some people call a sigh. This is key. Auditories will *hear* themselves experiencing the vacation, possibly having an internal dialogue with a native or traveling companion. They will experience the memories of that vacation primarily through sounds. Their breathing will get even more regular as they describe the pleasurable memories they have. If it was a beach resort they leisured at, they'll literally be hearing the waves crash against the shore. If they were away with friends, they might hear the conversations and laughs experienced with them at the time. And with typical auditories, as their eyes drift right and they deeply exhale—sigh—they might actually voice their thoughts about what they're hearing. If you listen closely enough, you'll be able to join them.

Voice

The breathing pattern of auditories will, quite naturally, affect the timbre and cadence of their voices. Also, when accessing dialogue, they will vary inflection depending on what sounds they're hearing. This produces a representational type that has no clear characteristic pitch. Undoubtedly, you'll notice how auditories project with much clarity, and not infrequently with a pleasing and listenable resonance. And because they are creatures of tone, you can be sure they succeed at being vocally precise and on cue. No lazy projection here. Although some auditories stop talking momentarily to access a new sound or to hear it first inside to audition it, a steady, rolling, even tempo is their trademark.

Musculature

Generally, auditories are not as tense or as slim as the typical visual, nor as muscular as the average kinesthetic. They exist somewhere between the two. I've seen enough variation in auditories to believe that they can appear in just about any form, so body style should be used only as the roughest guideline for identification.

Auditories can give you a clear indication of who they are through the use of *gestural accessing cues*, particularly with the use of their hands. While not as kinetic as the visual, auditories sometimes point directly to their ears while asking you to explain something. Recently I was having a difference of opinion—and a break in rapport— with a friend of mine. As we struggled to regain understanding, I remember his saying, "Don't you **see** what I mean? Can't you **see** how **unfocused** you're being? Try and take the **long view**, Michael." In my growing frustration to find some meaning in our exchange, I threw up my hands and exclaimed, "Yes! yes! I **see** what you mean"—and grew even more perplexed by his laughter, until I realized I was standing there with my index finger pointing to my *ear,* repeating, "I **see** what you mean! I **see** what you mean!" This specific gestural accessing cue is consistent with auditories or someone using his auditory representational system at that moment. Gestural cues also serve to stimulate the process of auditory accessing. Just as a catalyst in a chemical reaction helps along that reaction without actually becoming part of it, so the gestural accessing cue prods along the informational search. Another obvious cue is the cupping of one's ear while asking, "Could you repeat that?", which is a sure sign of an auditory. Gestural accessing cues are very revealing, probably because the conscious mind is not really involved in the process, and there is no editing of the gesture. Use these cues to supplement your skills in differentiating lead systems on the quest to establish rapport.

Eye Accessing Cues

Auditory eye accessing cues are fascinating to watch because they explain so much to the enlightened observer. Most of us have had the experience of talking with people whose eyes wander left and right as they engage us in conversation. It's not only distracting but apparently rude. Even worse is the offender who stares at you with a some- what defocused gaze that conveys the feeling of condescend- ing disinterest and boredom. We often react to this with distaste—and a sense that these people are totally de- tached. How interesting to find out that it's these very people who are the best listeners! They're auditory, and they are busy processing not only what you say, but what it sounds like to them and the meaning, through tones, that they assign to it.

An old friend of mine is a recording artist who was related to a man who served as her vocal coach. Having attained a good measure of success, he was some forty years older than I, and it always seemed weird to me that he was practically unable to keep any eye contact at all, especially while he was speaking. In fact, it was a family joke that he never really needed anyone there to talk with— just ask him a question and walk away. This was a source of great laughter for those around him, especially myself. I had no idea that he was an extreme auditory, and though it was hard for him to quit accessing his auditory neurology, he was a terrific listener. In fact, it wasn't until many years later that I realized he was the only person I knew then who would call up days later to reply to a question previously answered, but not to his satisfaction.

Auditories look directly to the right when they're put- ting a thought into words. When they do that, they're accessing either remembered (scanning left) or unfamiliar (scanning right) sounds. When they search for dialogue, however, their eyes *always* look lower left.

Because auditories cruise along at the level of sound, the way they operate in the world is necessarily different, at least experientially, from either kinesthetics or visuals. Auditories relate to their environment acoustically, thereby appreciating harmony or finding disharmony within their territory.

Auditories are emotionally sensitive, and their quest is always to be in harmony with a given situation. It's for this reason that auditories make wonderful negotiators and peacemakers. They thrive on bringing equilibrium to the equation and will offer unusually creative answers for tough questions.

Because of the nature of sound, auditories tend to hold on to their feelings for a longer period of time than, say, visuals. They like to work things out, even if it takes a while. This, of course, can drive some visuals to distraction, since images disappear quicker than sounds. Auditories do not dismiss relationships easily, and old friendships die hard. They have uncanny recollection of dialogue and are able to hear, years later, not only something that was said to them but the sound of the voice that said it! This explains why they are sentimentalists. Pop open a champagne bottle and the auditory in the room will respond to that unwitting reminder with a tear and be off to another period in time, experiencing, through sound, events of the past.

An auditory will contemplate a problem from a hundred and one different points of view, all the while sharing a dialogue with anyone around. If there is no one there, they are perfectly okay talking to themselves, thank you. When left alone with a puzzle, the auditory will hear it spoken from beginning to end, end to beginning, upside down, and inside out. And that's just for openers. They have the ability to reason through the way something sounds. This is because they're able to pull more information out of sound than the other representational types. It's akin to the way computers are able to get more significant data out of digital input than analog input. This will keep auditories hungry for another person to share their insights with, and they tend to make loyal friends. There is a very high probability of instant and long-lasting rapport between auditories. They seem to know each other immediately upon introduction and will soon be off enraptured by the sound of each other. They truly enjoy the nature of their rapport.

Auditories, alas, can ruminate about a love affair for an interminable amount of time after it has ceased to be. Words said between an auditory and her lover tend to stay fixed, and the bond created by that acoustical symmetry is a hard one to break. That's because auditory lovers "fit" very well with others. They tune in to another's exact frequency and endlessly get off on the rapport that's created. There's an enormous energy that's acquired from this joining, and when it's gone, when the love affair is over, even visuals can hear the hiss of steam that's released from the energy of the system. When this happens, the music leaves their lives, and only a new theme, totally unrelated to the first, will bring surcease. If left friendless, auditories will retreat to silence and try to rewrite the story of their life with fresh dialogue. A new love helps them along, but generally the auditory will carry the sound of his old love's voice with him for a long time. To love an auditory, one must learn the secret of silence...through harmony.

Auditories are an efficacious lot and their influence is all around: in the books we read (Ernest Hemingway), the movies we see (Steven Spielberg), and the people we laugh with (Johnny Carson); in our literary classics (William Shakespeare), through our war heroes and villains (Stalin); all the way up to great thinkers like Jonas Salk and Louis Pasteur, the auditory is forever a part of us. What these people share in common is that their auditory nature is observable even though they express themselves through other sensory channels. For example, Hemingway's writing obviously required visual pictures both externally, for him to see, and internally, for him to use as a synergistic comparison. This means that in his transderivational search* for the written word, he used pictures to draw sounds from. His writing is highly suggestive of the auditory type, both in its meter and through its use of auditory imagery. *For Whom the Bell Tolls* is a classic example.

Johnny Carson's wit revolves around the way he sounds. His strategy for being funny is auditory. When Carson goes for a line, he does a transderivational search for the best means of delivery, then checks it with how it makes him feel. If the internal sound makes him feel humor—that is, if it feels funny to him—his strategy is complete and he produces comedy. There is very little visual imagery to his comedic brilliance, especially when compared with that of someone like Steve Martin or David Letterman. Shakespeare's gift was also extremely auditory. His plays never really called for much visual staging. Recently, *MacBeth* played on Broadway and was criticized for its sparseness in staging. Naturally, this was important only to those critics who were visual. Shakespeare is really about sound; if you don't listen closely for minute variances in vocal inflection, meter, and even the twists of the words themselves, you will be lost. This is also the case with Steven Spielberg. Yes, I know it would seem that he's strongly visual, and I don't question that his movies depend heavily on visual imagery, but Spielberg engenders rapport with brilliant auditory skill. His works are laced with auditory cues. If you doubt this, think how E.T. sounded when he said he wanted to go home. Then imagine your experience of the movie without this auditory cue. Better yet, who but a true auditory could have imagined aliens arriving on Earth and using, as their

*A transderivational search is simply the mechanism we use to gain access to one representational system through the use of another. In Hemingway's case, he used pictures (the visual system), as "food" for thoughts, but he translated the images into sounds (the auditory system) as he penned his works—a common phenomenon.

very first gesture of communication with earthlings, the six tones in *Close Encounters of the Third Kind*. I'll bet you're hearing them right now!

More than visuals, auditories are easy to establish rapport with, probably as a result of their natural proclivity toward conversation. Many people report that auditories are approachable and make first meetings and introductions far easier for everyone. But joined with this attribute comes the responsibility of quick judgment and evaluation. When harnessed, this ability can enhance the auditory's power of assessment and sincerity; but in the unenlightened it can provide tough barriers to rapport.

Following are two examples of rapportless exchanges. Do you recognize yourself somewhere in the scenes?

Your lover is auditory. It's the fall and you figure it's a great time for a trip. So, after making a concerted effort, you plan a weekend up north to watch the October foliage and moonlight in Vermont. From the time the weekend begins, though, you see your good idea slowly heading for disaster. Despite the fact that the leaves are particularly beautiful this year and the rolling mountains are bright with colors and swirling smoke, your lover is at first vaguely distracted, then overtly bored and annoyed.

That night, you wake to find yourself alone in bed. You get up and look around, your anxiety starting to rise, then you let out a sigh of relief as you discover him on the porch. Standing out there alone looking at the hills in darkness, his discontent is gone and he appears almost serene. You tenderly join him and ask if he's okay. He smiles and says, "Sure, honey. I'm just listening to the song of the mountains. You'd be surprised how much there is to hear out there tonight."

You're kinesthetic. Your boss, a classic auditory and the president of the East Coast division of your company, with whom you need to share a good rapport, finally invites you to his estate for a Halloween ball. You're thrilled to death and show up fashionably late, making a grand entrance. The food is delicious, the people are beautiful and bright, the music—well, you can't help feeling moved, maybe even sentimental, especially by the strings. As the evening progresses, you feel charmed by the whole affair, and as memories of your past come up you enjoy them and the sensory experiences they create.

Dreamy-eyed, you make for the balcony where some interesting people have gathered, and an attractive woman engages you in conversation. She is friendly and charming and you share with her how nostalgic you're feeling and how anybody sensing the space of the party would feel that way too, just being there tonight. She frowns, points to her ear, and tells you it doesn't sound that way to her. As she backs away from you and into your boss, she giggles and not so quietly says: "Who's the weirdo, sweetheart?"

Congratulations, you've just met your boss's wife.

The way in which auditories use language is closely linked with their thought process. This is an important point. One of the most beautiful parts of this phenomenon is its consistency. People use language that exemplifies their representational type. Auditories are certainly no exception; they use language that is congruent with their representational style. For example:

Tell me how you like it.

That's *clear* as a *bell*.

Can we *talk*?

Keep your *ear* to the ground.

Can you *hear* what I mean?

This *rings* true for me.

These process words are not only concise indicators of auditory representation and will assist you in identifying an auditory, but they can be used very effectively to establish rapport. In chapter 6, "The Language of Rapport," we're going to learn some very subtle but powerful mechanisms designed to ease us into high rapport with auditories.

Auditories. Those whose map of the territory is sound. They are different from visuals. They don't come from the world of images. They're distinct from kinesthetics, too. They don't need to *feel* whether something is in order; they need to *hear* if it is. They attach meaning to life patterns by hearing dialogue and adding narration.

They can have a lanky appearance, but body style is not as obvious as in a kinesthetic or a visual. However, their voices will betray them. Listen to them. Even if they're not the most perfect, they will use their voices to enchant you with rich timbre and lush intonation, especially when they tell you a story. They are not breathy, and they maintain a flowing, full-chested respiration with syncopated timing. They speak with rhythmic pacing, sometimes a little fast just to get the words out before they're replaced by new sounds.

Auditory eye movements are easy to identify. When asked a question, auditories look from side to side to hear sounds, either recalling them from the past or imagining new ones to delight themselves. They have one special eye cue: looking to the lower left. When they look there, auditories are generating an internal dialogue. Thinking about both sides of a story, they'll check this position to confirm the clarity of both points of view. You'll also notice them cascading through the other eye access cues, usually when they make a picture of or check how they feel about what you've just said. But they will spend the majority of their time in the auditory positions.

The auditory will hear you quite well and will indicate this through gestural accessing cues. The most common of these will be pointing to his ear when telling you to explain something or to come to the point. These gestures are not meant as a put-down; they are simply part of the auditory communication package. Those who know this are more likely to be in rapport with him.

Like all system processors, the auditory's are highly

illustrative. "I **hear** what you're saying"; "That's as **clear** as a **bell**"; "**Sounds** good to me"; and "The **tone** of this conversation..." are common examples. Hear these, and know this person is an auditory or has shifted to the auditory mode.

Naturally, their lovemaking is not only auditory but audible. Use this as a particularly good way to achieve rapport. Encourage the communication of sex as a means to gratify their need to hear you. Responding to them with intimate sounds and dialogue will enchant them and put them under your spell. Remember, though, being auditory also means having an appreciation for silence. Though they will let you know what their threshold is for auditory stimulation, let loose with them! They really want to hear you!

Auditories love the symphony, so take them to a concert, but make sure it's one that's melodic and not discordant. Over supper, though they may not be conscious of it, the sound of the dinner music can determine their mood for the rest of the evening. Understanding this will make you a joy for them to be with. If I could choose just one present to give an auditory, it would be wind chimes. They're wonderful, and auditories just cherish them. Auditories gravitate to them as visuals to sunsets. They act as a tranquilizer and auditory relaxer. In fact, they're so effective in providing a sense of well-being and rapport I created a special wind chime for a close auditory friend.

Want to enthrall your auditory? Give her tastes of auditory stimulation through the sounds of the mountains, a running brook, even the likes of Springsteen. Combine city and country to challenge his sense of auditory discrimination. Bring the sounds of the waves into the bedroom. Better, take your auditory to hear the songs of the great whales, then watch the look of bliss on her face while listening to Gregorian chants. Follow this person wherever the music takes her.

Whispering to an auditory can enroll you in him forever. Whispering is the secret code to a lock of the auditory sense. Use it wisely and sparingly. Anchor your auditory (see chapter 10, "Anchoring"), to a sequence of personal whispers, then fire them off at the perfect moment. And be creative. Vary the melody or harmony. Keep a step ahead by changing keys and tones. And don't be afraid to be flat or sharp. Your auditory will love you for the variety. In chapter 10, you'll learn a particularly terrific way of doing this!

Finally, *give the auditory in your life the time to hear you.* Know that she is considering not only every word you say, but how it's said and with what emphasis. Auditories are internalizers, so let them have a few extra moments of internal conversation before expecting a reply. By doing this, not only will you understand your friend better and garner her appreciation for it, but you will have started to mirror her so harmoniously that you'll have begun the process of instant rapport.

Hear what I'm saying?

5

THE KINESTHETIC REPRESENTATIONAL TYPE

F you prize sensitivity above all else—and I mean above *everything*—the kinesthetic individual is someone you should get to know. These people long to be understood and respected for being so in touch with their feelings. Kinesthetic or feeling people will dazzle you with their innate ability to re-create *your* experience of joy, love, hurt, happiness, sadness, and gladness. They love to feel. Anything. Just don't take away their feelings. When they laugh, it's right down to the gut, giving you a sense that they totally understand and agree with what you think is funny. For the most part, they truly enjoy being in rapport because it gives them a solid ground of being to feel from—a kind of sensory base from which to form a new relationship that might produce fresh, new, and therefore unexplored feelings and sensations.

It would be hard to imagine life without these feeling-oriented people, and everywhere we travel their imprint can be found. They are the yin to the visual's yang. They are the interpreters of auditory dialect. They translate visual images and acoustical data into feelings that are pertinent to them and those around them. If not for kinesthetics, our lives would be two-dimensional, neither textured nor smooth, and when we related, it would be without benefit of emotional challenge. Kinesthetics supply the world with the poetry of who we are and how we feel about what we've done.

Kinesthetics enjoy conversation but not for the same reason visuals or auditories do. They use dialogue to transform words, sounds, and images into feelings. They are truly fluid about the creation of sensation from other sensory input. This works for them in a delightful way, and allows them to map out their territory through feelings. While visuals and auditories are busy communicating with pictures and sounds, the kinesthetic is busily running through his vast storehouse of feelings and attaching sensory meaning to what we've just said. Obviously, this trait can be both beneficial and detrimental. On one hand, humans enjoy the singular God-given miracle of emotion. It can heal us, fine-tune us to the universe of experiences we create, and be a striking copilot in our search for both structure and order within the context of our lives. On the other hand, emotions can keep us stuck in a cognitive loop of feelings that flies in the face of reason and logic. Kinesthetics are really incredible at accomplishing both.

Because of a heightened ability to feel, kinesthetics tend to be attracted to occupations that support their use of kinesthesia. When I first studied kinesthetics, I assumed they would be introverted and emotionally withdrawn. However, nothing could be further from the truth. Moreover, because of their superior sense of touch, kinesthetics make outrageous athletes! Any occupation that requires manual tasks is just plain easier for the kinesthetic. Typical occupations that are tailor-made for them usually have hands-on or feeling parameters. Psychologists, woodworkers, potters, surgeons, actors, all types of mechanics, and other feeling-

or sensory-based work are common callings. Also, kines-thetics are superlative linguists. They seem to be automati-cally ahead of the game when involved in an area that either depends on or is enhanced by the use of feeling.

If our primary representational system is kinesthetic, we're in touch with the world through feelings. We sense when things are good or bad. We get feelings about whether what we're doing is appropriate. In the big city or in a forest thick with trees, the kinesthetic will always be touch-ing his environment, relating to it through his feelings. It had to have been a kinesthetic who, by getting an innate sense of unification, originally assigned gender to inani-mate objects. Only someone coming from a sensory base of feeling could name a boat or a hurricane *she*. One of the world's most famous psychologists, Carl Jung, an obvious kinesthetic, referred to his own anthropomorphic creation, the anima, as "she who must be obeyed."

Kinesthesia is the representational system that permits us to attach sensation and feeling to our experiences. And as you know by now, all of us use our sense of feeling even though we may be strongly visual or auditory. From time to time, we all use our secondary systems in addition to our primary system representations, to do specific things. Kin-esthetics are no exception. They undoubtedly have specific behavior repertoires that are very auditory or visual. What I'm trying to say is that people who are kinesthetics don't operate out of feelings and sensation for *everything* they do. They let their other senses dominate for specific behaviors that vary from person to person. For instance, the kines-thetic woman who experiences the world through feeling, but is attracted to men primarily through how they sound; or the kinesthetic man who enjoys his sensory-filled work life yet relaxes by painting. They still experience most of their world through how they feel, but sometimes they use their other representational system for specific, particular tasks. Always keep this in mind when relating or communicating with someone with whom you want to be in rapport. It will give you a better understanding of why people behave the way they do and will help train you to expand your natural powers of sensory acuity.

Now that we know something about these feeling-based people, let's go a step or two further by examining a more complete outline of what to expect when meeting a kinesthetic. What signposts give an indication that we're relating with a kinesthetic? What can we expect a kinesthetic to look like? Talk like? And which information can we use to join them in deep rapport?

Physical Manifestations and Body Types of the Kinesthetic

Breathing Style

Have you ever had a conversation with someone who is so intent upon what you're saying that you can see their breathing kind of slow down and deepen? Most likely you were talking with a kinesthetic who's been reaching for a feeling about what you've said. These people tend to breathe low in the stomach area or diaphragm. They breathe deeply, as is logical for someone who is going through feeling changes, as opposed to auditory or visual change. The pace of their inhalation and exhalation is metered and thoughtful. As they bathe themselves in how their thoughts feel, their respiration changes correspondingly.

Because of their affinity for feeling, kinesthetics settle into this customary breathing pattern rather often, and this helps us identify them. I think we've all seen two people, maybe sitting on a couch away from the main fracas of a party, quietly chatting. The one who looked the most entranced by the other's words was probably a kinesthetic. They're wonderful empathizers because of their ability to replicate another's experience of feeling into their own, therefore truly re-creating for themselves the way another feels.

You can stimulate a kinesthetic into demonstrating her breathing pattern by asking questions that require her to represent experience kinesthetically. An example of this would be: "How do you feel about your marriage?" or, "Have you ever loved and lost?" The true kinesthetic will begin, sooner or later, to pull breath from the lower belly as he considers the wealth of feeling states that are internally generated in response.

Voice

Kinesthetics tend to have low-pitched voices, as one might expect from the way they breathe and the origin of their breath. For the most part, this is a pleasant attribute that these empathetic people share. To me, their voice pitch is actually a perfect match to their representational system. It just wouldn't feel right for someone who is so feeling oriented to have a staccato, shrill way of talking. They speak reassuringly, in a deep tonality that can inspire trust and confidence.

On the other hand, there is a tendency among these people to speak slowly, sometimes including long pauses in their sentence structure as they access information kinesthetically. This may be hard for an active visual to handle for a protracted period of time. At worst, this slower time frame combined with a sameness of pitch may be interpreted by an auditory as a soporific monotone. Be that as it may, it's not hard to like someone who is obviously in touch with how we feel. Most people consider that a hard-to-find quality.

Musculature

The kinesthetic body type is, like both the visual and the auditory body types, formed partially as a result of the individual's most highly valued representational system. Since kinesthetics position themselves toward areas in life where touch is important, it shouldn't surprise us that a typical kinesthetic body tends to be lean and muscular. This doesn't mean that all kinesthetics are body builders. What should be clear is that it makes sense for touch-oriented people to gravitate toward behaviors that satisfy their need for tactile stimulation. In our society, a good deal of these behaviors are related to manual labor, crafts, and sports. Hence, it would appear that kinesthetics tend to be "harder" and more muscular than, say, auditories, who don't require pulling and pushing and don't have a general desire to make physical contact.

In fairness to kinesthetics, though, I should point out that they sometimes appear to have fuller and softer bodies if their kinesthetic orientation is not externally tactile but internally visceral. By this I mean the difference between feeling that is internally generated—such as how we feel *about something*—and feeling that is externally generated— such as how someone or something *physically feels*. Some kinesthetics primarily generate internal feelings and don't depend much on their physical sense of touch, so you would perhaps expect them to be less toned than those whose feelings are generated more externally by touch. If you derive pleasure out of a heightened sense of touch, you will interact more with your physical environment, thereby altering the tone of your body.

Eye Accessing Cues

The eye accessing cue of the kinesthetic is simplicity itself. Much like their general presentation, which champions the law of simplicity and grace, kinesthetics have only one singular eye movement to indicate that they are accessing the kinesthetic representational system. When you challenge their feeling access with a question such as, "How do you feel about winning the game?", they will, under most conditions, look to the lower right.

When we talk with anyone, it's a sure bet that something about us or something about what we've said will produce a feeling response. Even the extreme visual will tap in to his sense of kinesthesia as a reaction to highly charged verbal input. But with kinesthetics, this is, of course, more a rule than with the other two primary systems. Kinesthetics will get a feeling about almost everything you say or do. They take this feeling and from it make a picture or hear a dialogue about the subject. But first and foremost is feeling. And as they access this feeling, their eyes look down and to the right.

Though visuals take the prize for being poorly understood, kinesthetics are often the unwitting recipients of misjudgment. There is a tendency in our society to categorize people who are in touch with their feelings as overly sensitive, and this in turn further propagates the idea of the kinesthetic as too emotional and soft. When we think about sensitive people, some of us see them as overtly emotional and verbally open about their feelings. As a result, though we know them by type, the kinesthetic has become something of a chameleon-like entity, never quite knowing whether it's in or out to show emotion. At various times it has been either avant-garde or unfashionable to be kinesthetic, producing popular attitudes of either misjudgment or misalignment. So society has had somehow to hold in perspective the feeling-based generation of the flower child while also catering to—even embracing—the drill-instructor machismo of yet a different time.

Kinesthetics are fiercely brave souls who will go to any

length to defend honor and reputation. They are surefooted as opposed to being swift and can exhibit tremendous staying power. Sometimes people confuse this with stubbornness, but that's inaccurate. Kinesthetics won't take a position before they check it with their feelings, and will abandon their position if it doesn't agree with their sense of things. Oftentimes others confuse this with not having a point of view, but this too is an inaccurate perception. Kinesthetics stay true not to how something looks or the way it sounds but to how they feel about it. Obviously, they are loyal, almost to a fault.

If anything is terribly active with these people, it's their emotional life. Because they operate out of feeling, they can, at any point, be charged with turbulence. They will replace feeling with feeling, and though they don't scatter themselves with quick emotional changes, the voltage of their heightened sensitivity will, at times, drain them. When they experience joy, it is the most pure form of ecstasy. If you are good friends with a kinesthetic you know this to be so, as the good feelings are wonderfully contagious and kindheartedly seductive. When they are light and breezy they will soar like an eagle—but sometimes they crash and burn.

The dark side of the kinesthetic can be most disconcerting and will drive visuals crazy. One of the great pitfalls of kinesthetics is their inability to exit a negative feeling strategy. It's very frustrating to observe a kinesthetic continually looping from sadness to depression about the sadness, to being more sad about the depression, and then even more depressed about their sadness... and so on. It's at times like this when a visual can be of assistance simply by asking the kinesthetic to make a picture of which state they're in. This will anchor the kinesthetic to one feeling state, where they can either linger or make a *choice* to move on to another.

Kinesthetics are lovers. They're terrific in bed because of the plethora of sensations that can be created there. In fact, kinesthetics can literally drift away during sex, entwined in their own cocoon of sensory delight. Further, this can become so intense that their lover may become incidental to the actual experience. This is where an auditory with good rapport skills can be very effective because, interestingly enough, many kinesthetics will respond to sound produced from strong feeling. An auditory can bring back a kinesthetic lover from his sensory moonwalk by gently talking him back down to the here and now with words wrapped around feelings of tenderness.

Because of the way they represent experience, kinesthetics react to falling in love and being loved with deep emotional states that can affect them and those around them. They tend to go through their feeling states often, so as to keep them grounded and anchored to the situation at hand. Within the context of a relationship, the kinesthetic will look into his current feeling state to check how he feels toward his mate, and will make a course correction by comparing how he once felt with how he is feeling presently. If a kinesthetic chooses to make a correction, he might let the memory of a perfect love influence the not-so-perfect feeling at hand. This can be a wonderful strategy for long-term commitment. As a matter of fact, a colleague of mine uses just such a strategy with his wife. These two vibrant people tend to challenge each other a lot and get pretty intense. He told me recently that when he gets really ticked off at her, he automatically makes a mental picture of the day he found her, and this triggers a feeling of love and appreciation. Because this simultaneously re-creates the condition of rapport, their relationship is not only salvaged by this but actually reenergized and refortified. By the way, this is a perfect example of what I mean by being able to stay in rapport with someone though disagreeing with the verbal portion of his communication.

It's not too difficult to notice kinesthetics in social situations, as they will usually give you more than enough time to speak your piece, and can be counted on to go that extra yard while considering your viewpoint. They are not very difficult people to share rapport with, yet we sometimes relate to them as though feelings and sensations were something recently brought to Earth by alien visitors. Do the following seem familiar?

You're visual. It's the first day of the semester, and everyone's a little nervous about the professor due to his reputation as a brilliant writer. There is a sense of challenge, though, and you can see from the looks on the other students' faces that it will be a terrific time for learning new techniques about your craft. "What a way to start off the new year," you tell yourself.

Your professor, kinesthetic as all get-out, enters the room. As he glances around, acknowledging with a warm and obviously shy smile those who have enrolled in his course, you tighten up with excitement and lean forward to watch him write the instructions for the first assignment. Except there are no written assignments and no words of instructions to read such-and-such a book. Instead, he asks you how it feels to be the first one to share your feelings on the group process. Looking down at his right hand while taking a slow, deep breath, he asks if you could give him a perspective on what it is you want to touch on for this learning experience.

You blush, look up and to the right for a picture of yourself with a smiling face, and in a quick, excited statement animated by gestures to all, reply, "I'm looking forward to seeing my skills as a writer improve along with the group's. And I want to see my writing take on a new frame of clarity and focus."

You start off the school year on the receiving end of the most confused look anyone has ever given you.

You're kinesthetic. But the guy who's stolen your heart isn't. It's been a few months, and while being with him has been super, the times when things aren't, have, for some unexplainable reason, been a drag. Somehow, when it comes to critical points along the way, either you or he can't quite make things fit.

It's your birthday and he lovingly, over a luscious dinner, presents you with a bright blue Tiffany box. You're delighted, of course, but as your eyes take in the brightness of the box, a tiny feeling in your gut says, "Uh-oh."

You undo the bow, apprehensively remove the cover, and (ta-da!) there are the brightest, most highly polished blood-red earrings you could ever imagine. When you touch them, they give you the feeling of starkly smooth ice.

Sure you love him, but let's face it, can you make it work over the long haul?

We've all had kinesthetic interactions like these. But now it's becoming easier for us to observe what went wrong in each case. Clearly, kinesthetic rapport was noticeably absent. We can achieve it by utilizing the technologies for its development. And as we're learning, one of the first clues we have to what representational group someone belongs to, and hence what guide we should follow to initiate rapport, is easily found just by observing language.

The kinesthetic uses processors that are indigenous to feelings. "I have a gut **feeling**"; "I **sense** you're right"; and, "Let's get a **handle** on things" are just a few examples of this. In chapter 6, "The Language of Rapport," we'll learn about "processors"—words that offer the discovery of people's representational systems—and how they are easily used to bring about rapport.

Let's see if we can condense what we've learned about the kinesthetic into a composite to serve as a general description. If we could script a scene composed of kinesthetic characteristics, how would it be? Would we recognize the kinesthetic at a convention or on vacation? How about at the office or on a date? Don't know yet? Then follow along.

With the exception of when they are accessing a feeling

and have a sudden increase in locomotion, the body movements of a kinesthetic are usually slower than that of either the visual or the auditory. More often than not, the deep tonality and breathiness of kinesthetics lend them an air of studied carelessness. They have fuller and sometimes harder bodies than visuals do, and can often take on the appearance of a great thinker.

The kinesthetic individual will clearly access the lower-right-eye position with much greater frequency than will a visual or an auditory. You can test this quite easily by asking a question that would require a sensory response, such as, "How are you feeling?" The kinesthetic will access that part of her cerebral hemisphere by orienting her eyes down and to the right. This stimulates the upper left brain, which is the part that controls feelings.

Kinesthetics like to think of themselves as the lovers of the world. And they're not far from correct. Because they translate all incoming data into feelings, they will respond to a situation more by how it feels to them than by how it may look or sound. You would think they'd make poor strategists, but they are delightfully innovative in their approach to seemingly nonsensory-based activities. I actually know a mathematician who is kinesthetic! His strategy for finding roots of differential equations is to assign feelings to visual mathematical notations and deduce the solution by *how it feels* to him. And judging from the writings of a personal hero of mine, Dr. Stephen W. Hawking—probably the most noted physicist of our time—I would venture to say that though he seems to be highly kinesthetic, he depends heavily on visual imagery to communicate his thoughts on quantum theory and relativity.

The way to a kinesthetic's heart is largely through his feelings. He usually has a sizable empathy quotient and will reason things out with you via sensation. Listen to the kinesthetic and you will hear poetry of the soul. I have found that it is wise to get a kinesthetic's viewpoint on any important decision. If you let them, they will help you get in touch with your own feelings—a part of you they understand totally, perhaps even better than you do yourself.

Since visuals and kinesthetics are at such opposite positions, one would assume that a relationship between them would require work. That would be a correct assumption. But let this not blind you to what can be done to promote wonderful friendships between the two. In a sense, kinesthesis is the original lead system. Long before our visual society was born—even before the society of the radio and phonograph was around—our ancestors depended heavily on sensation and feeling. Deals were cut on the basis of how things felt, not on the way they looked on paper or sounded in speech. So one might conclude that those who are primarily kinesthetic are the most evolved. After all, what's the point of a beautiful sunset or a moonlight sonata if it doesn't create a feeling within our hearts? It's hard to say. But I'm pretty certain that if you ask a kinesthetic his opinion, he'll tell you he has a gut feeling that you've touched on the truth.

PART II

The Technology of Rapport

6

THE LANGUAGE OF RAPPORT

L ANGUAGE is a terrific indicator of our representational systems. No matter where we go, representationally speaking, our language follows. Because we think in pictures, sounds, and feelings, our language should bridge the gulf between the internal representation of experience and the external delivery of it. If it didn't, others wouldn't have a way of knowing what we're experiencing at any given moment. And fortunately for us, it does. This is important to fulfill a major criterion of rapport: for us to be in rapport with others, we must understand how they represent reality in their own experience. Their language highlights how they think. Though we often tell people, "Do as I say, not as I do," we're much more consistent in our representative thinking. Maybe a more appropriate maxim would be: "Listen to my language, not what I'm saying."

The adjectives, verbs, and adverbs we unconsciously choose in speaking reveal which of the representational systems are highest in our consciousness. These "process" words, or *processors* as I'll call them, are language cues and will literally reflect what sensory channel someone is communicating through. People tend to use these processors in a highly ordered system, which reveals to the observer which way individuals are representing experience at the moment.

In our day-to-day lives, we use our representational systems in everything we do. And because we're multisensory, even though we may be, let's say, highly kinesthetic, we also make use of our vision and hearing. We often blend representational systems to make the most out of a particular experience. It's akin to seeing three-dimensionally or in color. In this way our experience becomes richer and more textured with stimuli.

Our internal representations of the world are so strong—indeed, they're our only connection to it—that we not only depend on them to represent experience but base our communication of that experience on the representations themselves. Simply put, we talk with people in the same language as we think. So if we're visual, and experience the world through light and form, we'll communicate visually, using language that is visual in nature. Let me give you an example of this:

I want you to **see** something.

Do you **see** how **clear** it is?

That's a really **bright** idea.

Let's **focus** in on that point of **view**.

Now that's a horse of a different **color.**

We must keep that in **perspective.**

Let's take the long **view.**

Can you **picture** what I mean?

That's a **colorful** way of putting it.

I know that at first this seems too simplistic to be viewed as hard fact. And at first, some people react to this concept quite skeptically. It just seems too easy, too literal. But that's precisely the point. Our language *is* literal. Especially when we describe experience. We talk in processors that reflect the representational system we're relating through.

It's probably obvious to you by now that if this is so, ascertaining someone's leading representational system should be a piece of cake. In fact, it's not only a piece of cake, it's pretty much the whole cake. The implications of this statement for instant rapport are quite strong:

> **We can identify someone's leading representational system by observing with what process words they communicate.**

You mean it's possible to learn how someone represents the world, or reality, to herself just by discerning what process words she uses? You bet. Like most of the technology of rapport, this technique is joyfully easy yet powerfully effective. It's easy because we're making use of a naturally occurring phenomenon that lets us search another's language for their road map of the world. It's powerfully effective because, almost by itself, it creates rapport.

> **People immediately feel more comfortable and in rapport with someone who's responding to them in the same language representations as they've communicated at that point in time.**

This dynamic technique is not only effective, but very elegant. When something is elegant, it creates the greatest results with the least expenditure of energy. In fact, matching someone's process language to create rapport is so elegantly effective, all you need to do is switch your gears, and keep your fingers out of the machinery.

If you know someone who organizes his experience kinesthetically, which of the following statements would be typical of that person's verbal communicative style?

1. I'd like to go to the beach today; how does that **sound** to you?

2. I'd like to go the beach today; is that something you **feel** like doing?

3. I'd like to go to the beach today; do you **see** any reason we shouldn't?

Obviously question 2 is kinesthetic, question 1 is auditory in nature, and question 3 is clearly visual. It doesn't get very much more complicated than that. Here's another example:

1. I love you so much, sweetheart, I can **see** us together forever.

2. I love you so much, honey, I know I'll be **saying** that forever.

3. I love you so much, darling, I **feel** like we'll be together forever.

Note the chart below, which elaborates on what I call *processor equivalents*. Each word is compared to its equivalent in the other representational systems.

Visual	Auditory	Kinesthetic
see	hear	feel
look	listen	touch
bright	loud	pressing
picture	sound	feeling
colorful	melodious	exciting
illuminate	be heard	be felt
clear	harmonious	fits
dawn	tune in	firm
flash	crescendo	spike
appear	discuss	aware
perspective	expression	hands-on
focused	listenable	secure
foggy	off-key	clumsy
strobe	harsh	irritate
form	resonance	angle

Matching Language and
Creating Rapport

When we understand how people organize their experience into the three representational systems, we can begin to see how valuable this is when utilized as a means of creating rapport.

The creation of rapport comes about when people get a sense that you understand them; that you're on the same wavelength. When we return communication that is generated in the same representational system in which it was delivered, we begin to speak the other person's language. Those of you who've traveled undoubtedly have had the experience of being in a country where the dialect is totally foreign. If you don't understand the language, it can be uncomfortable—even unnerving. Remember the feeling you got when you asked a stranger how to get back to your hotel, and he looked at you with a blank expression? For all intents and purposes, you were alone. Totally. You didn't get certainty from anyone that you were understood. Let me ask you this: Did you feel at ease and trustful? Could you have leaned back, kicked your shoes off, maybe closed your eyes, secure in fact that you were supported by others who knew you and where you were coming from? Of course not. In fact, not only were you out of rapport, you were out of luck—unless you had the good fortune to happen upon someone who spoke your language. Then what took place? Do you remember how you suddenly relaxed, took a deep breath, and painted a relieved smile across your face? Can you recall how safe and secure you suddenly felt, content with the knowledge that you had finally found a friend? Well then, if you've experienced this in one way or another, you can begin to understand how relating to someone in her representational language is akin to finding someone who comprehends and communicates in your native tongue.

> Matching representational processors immediately creates the condition of rapport.

When you match the system-specific words someone uses, you create a condition of rapport. In addition, you will be much better understood than when using process words that don't match. Mismatching your partner is a recipe for thwarted intention and is a terrific way of keeping rapport at arm's length. For example:

HUSBAND: I don't **see** why we have to go tonight.

WIFE: I keep **telling** you we have to.

HUSBAND: I just can't **picture** what could be so important.

WIFE: I've **told** you a hundred times, don't you **hear** me when I'm **talking**?

HUSBAND: Has it ever **dawned** on you that it's short-**sighted** to make plans without letting me know about them?

WIFE: What are you **saying**?

HUSBAND: Don't you **see** what I mean?

Engendering rapport by way of matching language, while technologically simple, is very effective. If a person's model of the world is auditory and they're asked a question that assumes visuality, by its very nature the dialogue produced will be out of sync, out of rapport—pretty much like our example above. However, when we match processors, system to system, we're coming aboard someone's lay of the land. We're talking in a language they not only understand but feel comfortable with.

Let me demonstrate both sides of the coin in one story:

It's just before dinnertime and Marc arrives home. Behind his back, are a dozen roses he bought downtown not twenty minutes ago. He can't wait to see Kim, the woman he's crazy about and has been living with for the last two years. Things have been good with them except for the fact that Kim has been "overly sensitive" lately and doesn't think Marc tells her enough that he loves her. Marc disagrees with this, claiming to be a very demonstrative man.

As he walks through the door he tries to wipe the smile off his face. Hiding the flowers behind his back, he waltzes into the living room.

Mismatched and Rapportless

MARC: Honey, I'm home.

KIM: (walking out of the den) Hi, sweetheart. (Reaches up, then kisses him.)

MARC: Jeez, you **look** great, Kim. New blouse?

KIM: No, just haven't worn it for a while.

MARC: (grinning from ear to ear) Here, sweetheart, just for you (hands her the flowers). Aren't they **bright** and **pretty**?

KIM: (half smiling and looking lower left) Oh, yes, they're lovely (bringing the flowers up to her **ear** and **chuckling**), and they're **purring** like kittens with happiness. How thoughtful, Marc. I love you.

MARC: You seem **radiant** tonight, Kim. It's so good to come home to you (looking up and to the left, then to the right). You know, we really do make a great-**looking** team.

KIM: (bursting into tears) You don't love me. You never **tell** me you love me. Do you think I'm **deaf**? Oh, you don't even **hear** what I'm **saying**, do you? (Runs into the bedroom while Marc stares at the flowers and wonders what's going on.)

Familiar? You bet. But what's happening here? Has Kim taken leave of her senses? Has Marc been "insensitive" again? Well, if we examine the complete picture, it becomes clear that we've got two different primary systems at work, and they've each broken rapport. They're not in rapport because each is communicating in his *own separate* (representational) language. It's not very different from speaking Spanish to someone who understands Italian. Although they share similar roots, meanings and differentiations will be quite disparate. What Marc and Kim need to do, of course, is to "talk" to each other in their *partner's* language.

As you are probably aware, Marc is communicating as he sees the world, because he's a visual person. Though he really does love Kim, he's visual and sees his love as clear as a picture. He relates to the world through images and can see himself loving her and how they look as a couple in love. This then gives him a feeling of being wanted, which in turn gives him another picture of loving Kim.

On the other hand, Kim, an auditory, is responding as she *listens* to the world, and can hear her love for Marc as clear as a bell. Telling her what it would sound like to love her would cause Kim to listen to him as a partner. Then asking her to notice if what he's saying rings true would create an internal dialogue enabling her to reach auditory satisfaction and rapport, just by following her language formula.

To create rapport, we match the process words of our partner.

When we match our partners' process words, not only are we speaking their language and being understood, but we're also relating *with* them as opposed to relating *to* them. This is because we're in the picture with them; we've become *associated*—seeing, hearing, and feeling life the way *they* do. Moreover, when our partner relates back to us in kind, through *our* representational system, we begin to ease up, unwind, and rekindle the reason we're with that person in the first place—attraction. Therefore, just through the process of communicating in the same tongue, we've not only made ourselves understood, but have also reclaimed the integrity of our heart's desire.

Following is a rewritten example of rapport-rich dialogue. You'll notice that Marc and Kim are merely communicating in each *other's* representational language. The words may not be the ones you would use, but we're really not talking about what you'd say; rather, about how it's represented. Again, I've highlighted the processors.

Matched and Rapport-Rich

MARC: Honey, I'm home.

KIM: (walking out of the den) Hi, sweetheart. (Reaches up, looks to the upper left, then directly at him.)

MARC: Jeez, you **sound** terrific. Had a good day?

KIM: Not especially. But it's so good to **see** you.

MARC: (grinning from ear to ear and humming *their* song) Here, honey, just for you (hands her a compact disk of *their* song). Remember where we were when we first **heard** it?

KIM: (with a big smile) How can I forget! We were at the old beach house. Remember how **bright** the stars were that night? I can still **picture** them. Can you **see** how much I love you, baby?

MARC: Kim, sometimes it's so **clear** to me that you do (looks from side to side, then at Kim). I love you, too, sweetie. Y'know Kim, we'll always be in **harmony.**

You'll notice that Marc and Kim have created rapport simply by speaking in each other's language. Marc is now communicating in Kim's auditory mode, while Kim is doing the same in Marc's visual mode. How incredibly simple yet effective this is. And it's really no big deal. When you model someone's representational dialect, you're truly promoting the establishment of rapport. Often, a natural trust will form from this process alone, and it'll just be something else you do in the normal procedure of getting to know someone. Establishing rapport linguistically is *not* Newtonian physics. It's just using technology to help us in our struggle to relate.

Do Marc and Kim love each other *the same*? Or in the *same way*? I don't know. What I do know is *that* they love and want to be together. This is one way of keeping the momentum flowing and building high rapport.

Sometimes, much to our chagrin as rapport builders, we'll run into people who have the nasty habit of occasionally not using descriptive process words. At first, this is inconvenient, and we might feel stymied. But only momentarily. When someone isn't coming from sensory experience, they tend to use digitized language—in other words, language that doesn't allow us to observe where they're coming from, representationally. Some examples would be:

I want to let you know something.

I understand what you mean.

Can you describe what you mean better?

My experience of last night was really nice.

When you do that, it isn't a nice thing.

I bought some good shoes today.

Did you like the story?

How much are you interested?

What these statements have in common is their lack of representational thought. There are few, if any, words highlighting internal process. Process words that do not specify which portions of internal experience people are coming from are called, quite naturally, "unspecified." They lack a well-formed sensory meaning. They present us with content only, and leave us either to surmise their meaning or to ask a question in reply to elicit more of the "meat" of the experience. One technique that I use to "tease" more sensory information is to ask, "Specifically." For instance, if someone says to me, "You know, I was really wild about her," I reply, "How, specifically?" Believe it or not, after being asked, people usually enrich their descriptions enough for us to pick out some sensory-based qualities, whether they're feelings, sounds, or pictures. But sometimes even that leaves us wanting, verbally. Which, not by accident, leads me to direct your attention to the following chapter, "Eye Accessing Cues." There, the universal language of eye patterns will lead us even farther along in our journey to instant rapport.

So far, we've learned that we can discern how people internally represent experience by an awareness of the system or process words they use. We've also learned that it's not only possible but actually natural and easy to establish rapport, simply by matching these words and offering them back.

In the following chapters we're going to combine linguistics with eye accessing cues, mirroring, strategy unpacking, and anchoring to produce states of rapport you never thought possible. And it's going to be a fun process, for the technology of rapport is rapport-rich itself.

7

EYE ACCESSING CUES

The eye obeys exactly the action of the mind.

—Emerson

W HEN I was a young boy, I had a terribly close friend named Mathew. He was a wonderful fellow and I remember with a special fondness in my heart how we used to run and play in the meadow and how close we were. One of the things I most enjoyed about him was his ability to paint a picture of something in his mind after a moment's pause. He had a knack for being able to concentrate and then come up with an exact picture of what he was thinking. I remember noticing that whenever he did this, he almost always looked upward, as if to see his forehead. I didn't know back then that he was literally seeing the picture just before he told me about it.

I haven't seen Mathew in a long long time, but I'll always remember him as my first visual friend. Long before I knew rapport-technology ever existed, Mathew was busily accessing his "remembered pictures." These are images that are recalled from the past just as they were originally seen. I couldn't have known it then, but Mathew was a true leading visual. His hands flew furiously as he spoke, and he was barely able to get the words out before the picture changed. Even at so tender an age, I knew that to keep up I would have to pace myself with him, so when we were together I did what he did. I entered his model of the world. I even used his favorite expression, "That's a horse of a different color," when something he did suddenly became clear to me. We got along famously. He was great fun, and I loved him dearly, but I was always exhausted when I got home from an afternoon with him. Some visual people can affect you that way. Yet, he was my closest boyhood friend and we had a wonderful friendship. I guess you could say that Mathew and I were in rapport.

We've all heard the expression, "The eyes are the window of the soul." If you looked close enough into someone's eyes, the implication is that you'd be able to see his true self. This is a wonderfully romantic notion and no doubt many films have made use of this lovely metaphor. Still, all of us have learned that looking into a person's eyes can hardly let us know what he's about. Or can it? Is it possible to get information about someone simply by looking at his eyes? And if so, can this information be used in a meaningful and productive way, such as assisting us in the creation of rapport? The answer is a resounding *yes!*

One of the neatest and, in my opinion, most significant models of behavior to come from neurolinguistic programming is the eye accessing cue. The wealth of pertinent behavioral information one can derive by the observation of eye movements is staggering. In fact, it usually comes as a shock to people that eye movement patterns are so powerful, they can often be used *alone* as means of establishing rapport. In my seminars, people consistently tell me how valuable this technology alone has been for them.

In this chapter, we'll explore eye movement patterns and train ourselves in their interpretation. At the completion of this chapter, you'll never again be at a loss to understand people's behavior; in fact, you'll be able to tell in what representational system someone is thinking. Moreover, you'll become so astute at this form of nonverbal communication that you will, at times, actually be able to know what someone else is thinking!

As we discussed in chapter 1, we all use accessing cues of many varieties to help us gain access to our internal states, thereby assisting us in getting in touch with an experience we either had or are presently having. In the chapter on visuals, for example, we briefly mentioned that when we talk and point with our hands to specific areas of our body, we're using gestural accessing cues. For instance, when someone scratches her head while answering a question or points to her ear when asking you to be more specific, she's demonstrating a gestural accessing cue. They're called *gestural* because they come about through gestures, usually with the use of arms and hands. Gestural cues, like all accessing cues, stimulate our search for a particular bit of information. Rather than *cause* an experience with feeling, sound or visuality, the accessing cue may be thought of like a catalyst in a chemical equation. The catalyst doesn't partake in the reaction, it simply *stimulates* the reaction to occur. In the same way, while not actually causing the visual, auditory, or kinesthetic experience, eye accessing cues stimulate our brain to access the particular representational behavior we're searching for. In doing so, these actions supply information to the trained observer about what representational system is being accessed at the moment.

However pertinent gestural accessing cues may be, the best of them pale when compared with the uncanny accuracy eye accessing cues provide. In fact, eye accessing cues have their own unique and specific formula for interpretation that is quite easily understood. But before we go into an explanation of them, let's have some fun by seeing what they look like.

Grab a friend and ask the following questions while watching his eyes:

- What does your bedroom look like?
- What color is your mother's hair?
- What did you wear yesterday?

Chances are, the person looked to the upper left when answering. Now ask another few questions:

- Do you love your boyfriend?
- If you were ever burned, what did it feel like?
- What was it like jumping into an ice-cold lake?

This time, there's a pretty strong possibility that he looked to the lower right when answering.

People use their eyes to help them access the experience you're asking them for. In the above examples, looking to the upper left allows them to *see* a remembered image much better. And looking to the lower right automatically helps them get in touch with how they *feel* about a particular experience. Looking to the lower right stimulates the part of the brain where we store our emotions regarding a particular stimulus. It's not really important for us to remember all the scientific jargon, as long as we know that eye accessing cues are valid and provide us with a reliable source of behavioral and rapport-rich information.

There is one caveat that I must bring to your attention, though. When we speak about eye cues going to the left and to the right, we are describing those eye movements as they apply only to right-handed people.

Left-handed people have the exact opposite response.

For example, a *right-handed* person will look up and to the **left** for the memory of a visual image, while a *left-handed* person will look up and to the **right** for the same visual memory. In another instance, a righty will look down and to the **left** to hear an internal dialogue, while a lefty will look down and to the **right** to hear the same information. *The up-and-down parts never reverse.* Only the left and right movements are reversed in individuals with left-handed dominance.

Because right-handed dominance is so pervasive in our culture, this presents hardly any problem at all. Ninety percent of those we communicate with are right-dominant. But am I saying to forget lefties? Absolutely not! In fact, as you get better and more confident as a result of practicing your observational abilities, you will get to a point where you'll know if someone is right- or left-handed just by watching her eyes. I mean it! You're going to get so good at this that it will come as second nature to ask someone a feeling question, and notice she's left-handed by watching her respond with feeling content while looking to the lower left; or by noticing that a lefty is answering a constructed visual question while looking in the visual remembered position. I know this might seem a tad confusing just now, but let me ease you with the certainty that all this information will fall into place.

On some occasions, you will find people not using their eye accessing cues. That in itself, of course, is a response. It's a challenge to a specific question or to their awareness of your obvious scrutiny. In our society, mimicking and very apparent observation of someone's behavior are not considered socially appropriate. Accordingly, people's response to close scrutiny is often an attempt at no response at all. So it's important to use discretion in your observation. Whatever you do, don't be confrontational. And don't be concerned about missing a glance here and there. Eye cues tend to be repetitive, and however long someone's particular accessing strategy is, it will probably be repeated at least a few times during the course of any communication.

And one other point. When we ask questions to elicit the eye accessing cues, remember that *everyone* will look to the appropriate eye cue in response to a corresponding question. That is, we'll look to the upper left to answer a question that demands a visual memory. And we'll look to the lower right for access to our feeling sense—*no matter what our primary representational system is.* The important thing to remember is that unless we're asked specific sensory questions which stimulate us to move our eyes to that respective sensory position; or we're accessing that position because of a specific mental search that we're processing at the moment, our eye accessing cues tend to stay pretty much within our primary representational area.

The following is a composite eye accessing cue chart. We'll break it down as we cover each eye position and define its significance.

Eye Accessing Cues

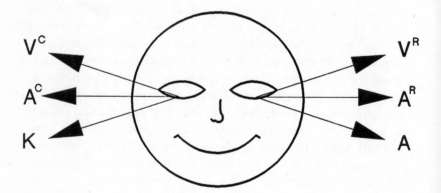

V^R: *Visual Remembered Images*: Images seen before, recalled in the way they were originally seen.

V^C: *Visual Constructed Images*: An image or picture of something not seen before.

A^R: *Auditory Remembered Sounds*: Words or sounds that were heard before.

A^C: *Auditory Constructed Sounds*: Words or sounds that haven't been heard exactly that way before.

A: *Auditory Dialogue*: Having an internal dialogue with yourself or others.

K: *Kinesthetic*: Sensations, feelings, and emotions.

Visual Remembered Images

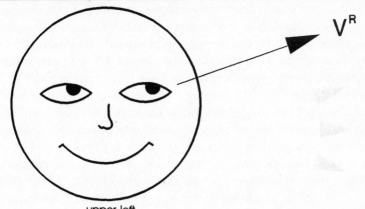

upper left

This is probably the most easily recognizable eye cue because it is so common in everyday life. We all have a picture in our minds of asking someone a question and seeing him respond by looking up, scratching his chin, and uttering, "Hmmm, let me see." Since so many people are visuals, this is one eye cue you'll see often. Even those who aren't primarily visual use visuality as a key part in many of their strategies and so will exhibit visual eye cues.

When people look up and to the left, they are accessing and searching for a remembered picture. They're trying to find an image of someone or something that they've seen before. The mind has an incredible way of storing these images and calling them up on demand. And looking to the upper left actually stimulates the visual part of the brain, helping us recall previously seen pictures. A lot of our behavior is based on our remembered images of past events, and we constantly compare the past part of our lives with the present or possible future. Because of this, the other visual eye cue—upper right, indicating constructed images (*those images never before seen*) is often observed either preceding or following the visual remembered cue. This ordinarily indicates that the person is comparing what she remembers with what's so for her presently or in the possible future. This is an asset when we compare something we did yesterday—that didn't work—with how to do it today, working perfectly. But be warned that this very same comparison can be a pitfall, as in the case of a flawed attraction strategy, where we compare a new love with an old and trusted one. In this strategy we get stuck in the past, idealizing what may have been an imperfect but comfortable union. We search each untested love possibility to see if our current picture—that of ourselves and our new love— fits our past picture of happiness and content rapport. What this often looks like in life is the classic choice of a mate based upon an inappropriate visual attraction strategy that has ceased to be useful for us.

When you talk with a visual, for the most part, she'll access the upper left and right eye positions. However, since we're made up of a mixture of all systems, you'll also notice visuals accessing the eye positions for dialogue and feeling. This can be common. What clearly differentiates a dominant visual is the *quantity* and the *frequency* of time spent in the upper positions. You'll sometimes notice visuals darting to the upper left and right visual positions very quickly yet infrequently. At other times you'll see them looking up during a large part of their conversation with you. It's been my experience that visuals (as well as auditories and kinesthetics) retain their specific eye cue patterns over the course of their lives. By patterns I mean individual preferences of duration. For example, visuals who spend a lot of time (duration) in the upper left and right areas tend to consistently exhibit *that* specific mode of eye movement. Likewise, those visuals who access upper left and right positions fleetingly tend also to retain *that* particular pattern over time.

If we want someone to access a remembered image for us, we need not do anything more than bring him into the visual mode. This is easily accomplished by asking questions, like those below, which stimulate the search for visual remembered pictures. These questions are strictly illustrative, however. They serve simply to demonstrate the validity of the eye accessing procedure, and may have no bearing on the specific uniqueness of another's criterion for rapport. In other words, visual questions will have people accessing visual eye cues even if they are auditory or kinesthetic. The actual content of the questions should be, obviously, within the context of what you want to find out at the time. Bringing about rapport by way of eye accessing cues will be explained throughout the book, in applicable and appropriate areas.

Notice how often people look to the upper left when responding to the following questions:
- What color is your mother's hair?
- What did your house look like when you first saw it?
- Who was the first person you saw today?
- Do you have a red sweater?
- What color are your father's eyes?

Visual Constructed Images

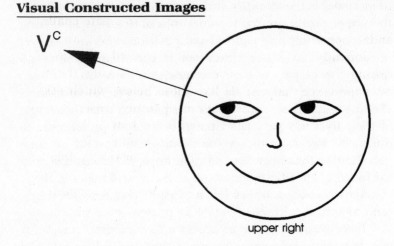

upper right

This is another easily recognizable eye cue because it, too, is very common. You've probably unconsciously noticed people looking to the upper right, on and off, during the course of a conversation. What you didn't notice is how this eye cue is paired to constructing or putting together an image or picture. We usually observe this eye cue when people are considering how something might look. It might be how they'll look tonight or what they'd do with a million dollars, or even what their next lover will be like. Because of a common cultural bias, we tend to generate more interest in images as they once were rather than how they will be. Accordingly, the upper right eye accessing cue might be noticed just a little less often than the upper left cue.

When we look up and to the right we're accessing a picture of someone or something we've either never seen or haven't seen in quite that way. In this fashion, we're able to get a glimpse of what the future might look like. Most people have a pretty good ability to do this, and those with terrific imaginations depend on their constructed images to keep that part of themselves chugging along. Many people run their lives as though their constructed images are all they have, while others use this facility to create challenge and opportunity for themselves.

Getting someone to access constructed pictures as a demonstration is strictly a function of asking the right questions. They should be like those below, which ask for visual information in the present or future tense.

- What would you look like with red hair?
- Can you picture a sunset with lightning?
- Can you imagine the Twin Towers in the middle of a meadow?
- Can you picture yourself in love with a mermaid?
- What would a safari look like?
- Can you see a polar bear flying a 747?
- What will tomorrow look like?

Auditory Remembered

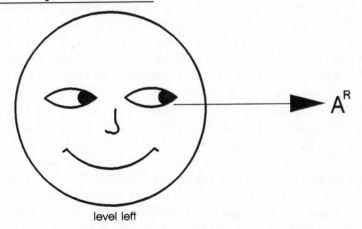

level left

Singing to yourself, especially a singular tune or part thereof, is a process we can all identify with. It's part and parcel of cycling through a remembered auditory loop and continually getting stuck on playback.

The remembered auditory eye cue is a level look to the

left. When we first begin observing eye movements, we must pay particular attention to this accessing cue. For some reason our brains don't register it as significant. Maybe it seems so natural that someone's quick glance to the side just isn't selected as outstanding. Yet, after you observe it in action and become aware of it, it's a hard one to miss. It's all in the training.

When a person looks to the left she is remembering sounds she's heard before. My favorite example of this is the sound of a freight train in the still of the night. This unique auditory anchor (see chapter 10) immediately stimulates our auditory remembered eye cue. Then it accesses our kinesthetic representations by producing a very strong feeling state. If you want to observe people accessing their auditory remembered eye cue, simply ask if they can recall how a freight train's whistle sounds. Some people will glance to the left quickly. Others will linger there. Those who remain or return to it quickly are probably dominant auditories. But even dominants will then cascade to the lower right kinesthetic eye position. This provides them with a feeling stimulated by hearing the freight train's whistle. This is known as a transderivational search. It simply means we use one sensory system—in this case the auditory stimulation from the train's whistle—to activate another sensory system: the *feeling* we get as a result of this sound. With many auditories, sound is the genesis of feeling. Understanding this will give you a terrific edge when communicating with an auditory. My friends who understand the importance of rapport know that relating to me is most effective for them—and intrinsically pleasing for me—when delivered with auditory care. And they grasp that when I'm glancing to my left, I can be reached easily through sounds and tones.

Producing an auditory state and thus demonstrating the auditory remembered eye accessing cue is simple. It's probably obvious by now that to do this, we ask questions to stimulate the auditory representational system. Remember, though, that observing someone in the auditory remembered eye cue doesn't necessarily mean he is auditory. It may just signify that he's in an auditory process at the moment.

Following are examples of questions that stimulate the auditory mode and will elicit the corresponding eye access cue:

What's your favorite melody?

How does your doorbell sound?

How does your favorite song go?

Does the sound of the surf seem familiar?

What does wood snapping in your fireplace sound like?

Auditory Constructed

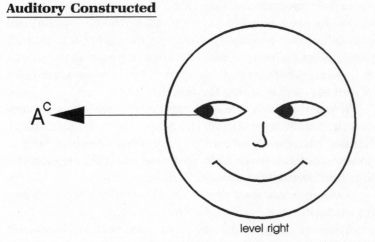

level right

When someone looks directly to the right, she is constructing an auditory experience. She might be imagining how she will sound tomorrow or how someone else will sound. She may be trying to hear a new sound such as her child's first complete word. When philosophers ponder the existential question, "What is the sound of one hand clapping?" they represent the answer as an auditory construction.

One of the interesting observations about this eye

accessing cue is that we often find it combined with its opposite, the auditory remembered cue. Have you ever noticed people who scan their eyes back and forth as they engage in conversation? They have a strategy for listening that consists of hearing unfamiliar auditory information, then quickly checking it against acoustical data with which they are familiar, and which is stored in their auditory memory.

We access auditory construction when we want to hear something we haven't heard before. If someone takes us to a concert featuring an artist we've never heard before, you can be sure we'll be checking our auditory constructed sounds on the way there. Locating specific words in sentences will produce the same kind of eye movement. Quick, what's the sixth word in our national anthem? Gotcha! Did you notice your eyes drifting over to the right? It's natural. And it gives us insight into building rapport with people. By knowing where someone is coming from representationally, we can sort of tag along for the ride.

When we put a thought into words we are also constructing auditorily. Often thoughts are nebulous things that don't have form or context. Using our powers of auditory construction, we're able to transform this experiential data into words that are intelligible to others.

Types of questions that elicit the constructed auditory eye accessing cue are as follows:

Can you imagine the sound of your next love's voice?

What could I say to make you hear that?

Can you hear your child's voice combined with a harp?

What's the eighth word in "T'was the Night Before Christmas?"

What's the sound of air hitting water?

Auditory Dialogue

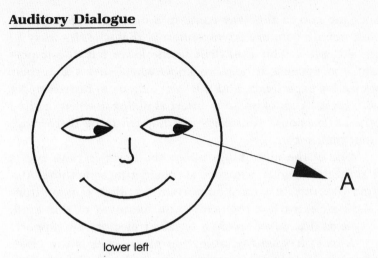

lower left

You're talking with an acquaintance by the entrance to the club. He's telling you about how terrific his day has been, how his new girlfriend is totally incredible, and how he beat the pants off the new vice-president of marketing in a two set tennis match. You're listening attentively, then realize the commencement of the usual dialogue in the back of your head—you know, that yamma-yamma that goes on and on forever? It runs something like this:

Sure, Steve, your day's probably been great because your boss's been on vacation for the last two weeks. And your girlfriend's that incredible? How obnoxious! The tennis match? Excuuuuuse me! What did you do, McEnroe, beat him into submission with your designer racquet? Jeeeez!

Well, that voice-over is called internal dialogue and holds a special position—auditory dialogue—in our chart. When we access our internal dialogue, we look to the lower left.

Internal dialogue is very important if you are auditory. Since auditories think in sounds as opposed to pictures or feelings, being able to discuss an issue with themselves is key. Auditories will hear both sides of a story via internal dialogue and in this way come to a decision. When you're with people who are having internal dialogue, it's easy to observe when their eyes drift to the lower left. It's important, too, because it helps us know where they are in their subjective experience, and this will help us to be in rapport with them. A lot of us go to internal dialogue when making critical decisions. Auditories just happen to be there more often than most.

One of the nice things about the lower left eye cue is that it tells us when someone is considering something. At a time like this, it's most important to allow our auditory friend an extra few moments. Consideration of this kind, simple as it is, places us in a terrific trajectory for rapport.

A most frequent combination of eye cues is the lower left dialogue position paired with the lower right feeling cue. People having internal dialogue will, from time to time, check their lower right cue to stimulate their feeling-based or kinesthetic representational system. This helps them come to a decision by checking *what* they're saying with how they *feel* about what they're saying. If their dialogue and feelings are congruent, they'll exit their strategy and make a decision based on the result of that strategy.

Questions that will stimulate a lower left dialogue search, and will demonstrate that eye cue, are:

Can you tell yourself a story?

Can you hear both points of view?

Do you talk to yourself when you read?

What do I really want to do in life?

Finish "Four score and seven years ago..."

Can you repeat to yourself what I just said?

Kinesthetic

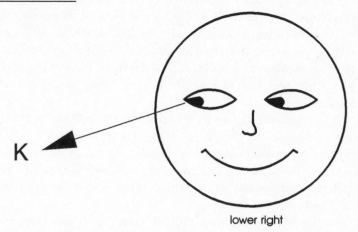

lower right

I love the kinesthetic eye accessing cue. It has so many nice qualities to it. First, it is simplicity personified. Just one simple direction representing one unified system. Second, it looks the way a feeling should look: kind of pensive and thoughtful, maybe even soulful. And last, but not least, it's not at all arbitrary, for the kinesthetic eye accessing cue is simply and plainly ...lower right. Period.

The kinesthetic cue will, of course, be seen most often when we are interacting with a kinesthetic. However, everyone displays this eye movement when attaching feeling to something. When we ask a person who's highly visual to picture his childhood home, it's a good bet he'll move his eyes from upper left to lower right, as he attaches emotional content to the picture.

Have you ever talked with anyone who stared away from you and toward the floor? Most likely they were accessing their feelings about something you'd just said.

It's been my experience that kinesthetics spend a lot of time in the lower right eye position. This might be due to the fact that feelings are not fleeting things, as are pictures or sounds, and it's a rare person who jumps from feeling state to feeling state continually, without pause. In fact, our society considers that kind of behavior bizarre. Kinesthetics tend to stay with a feeling, at least for a while, and can easily be observed deep in thought. One artistic example of this is the sculpture known as *The Thinker.* We are right on target when we classify kinesthetics as "being in touch with their feelings."

It is important to know when someone shifts into kinesthetic, because it shows us they are representing their experience emotionally, not with images or sounds. It's also important because it supplies us, nonverbally, with one complete component of whatever strategy is being used at the moment.

In the next section of this chapter, we'll see that eye accessing cues are more than just a nice formula for predicting eye movement. They are literally the road signs that point the way to rapport-rich and rapport-productive relationships.

Following are kinesthetic accessing questions that seek to stimulate the lower right eye cue, thus causing feelings and/or sensations:

- Have you ever been burned?
- Did you ever fall in love?
- Ever taken an ice-cold shower?
- What was it like diving off the high platform?
- Have you ever loved and lost?

Remember that kinesthetic questions will stimulate kinesthetic eye cues—*even in visuals and auditories.* And visual questions will produce visual eye cues—even in auditories and kinesthetics. And, of course, the same holds true for auditory questions—they will elicit auditory eye movements even in visuals and kinesthetics.

Now that we're clear about which representational system stimulates the eyes to move in which direction, and have a good understanding of their significance, let's move on to *Cascading* and the *Silent Strategies.*

Cascading

Very simply, this is the process whereby we shuttle from representational system to representational system and physically demonstrate it with corresponding, involuntary eye movement.

People are multisensory, and none of us uses just one representational system all the time. If we did, not only would we miss out on most of the incredible beauty our world has to offer, but we would certainly be handicapped. Indeed, that is what we call people who are not able to manifest the use of a particular lead system: handicapped. When we are not able to see, we are called blind. When we are not able to hear, we are called deaf. And so on. However, since God has blessed the majority of us with a fully functioning package of senses, we integrate this "sensory bundle" as we represent *to ourselves* the world in which we live. And so when we observe eye accessing cues, we must be aware that people will often jump from sense to sense in order to get a full experience of the richness of information they're searching for. In doing so, the eyes will follow the internal neurology of this search, and will move according to which sense or representational mode they are accessing at the moment. I call this "being in the moment of now." In any moment of now, we are accessing just *one* dimension of representation. In other words, we are accessing either our visual, auditory, or kinesthetic representational system. We are either seeing the information, hearing it, or having a feeling about it. As we *cascade* from each moment of now representationally, our eye cues follow by changing their position to correspond with the system we're utilizing at that moment. So when we ask someone to give us the eighth word in the Pledge of Allegiance, for example, we might see his eyes move to the left, to get the auditory memory of the pledge, and then to the right, to construct the auditory *sound* of the words so he can count them off to get to the eighth word. But we may first notice the person move his eyes to the upper left, accessing visual memory, to picture what the pledge *looked* like; and then back to the left and right to complete the auditory access search. Additionally, we may observe the person executing the previous components of the cascade, then following it with a third component of looking to the lower right. This will demonstrate that he is accessing a feeling about something—possibly about what the pledge means to him. Then again, this little drama can take place *in any order*, the relevance and beauty of which will serve you enormously when you want to figure out someone's strategy for attraction or buying or arranging the perfect weekend or any other specific behavior. Because if you know how to fulfill someone's criteria for a successful task, in essence you have begun the process of instant rapport.

Cascading is not some weird phenomenon you'll see once in a while. It happens practically all the time and is a natural manifestation of our experience. We constantly move from one representational system to another as we react to our experience of life, even though we consider ourselves oriented primarily to one system. If we're visual, for example, though our primary map of the territory is through images, we also use our senses of hearing and touch not only for specific tasks but, as noted earlier, for a "well-formedness" of experience. Even if we are totally visual, we don't abandon our other senses. In a way, it's kind of like playing tennis or putting on makeup—even like shaving— because though these tasks require lots of visuality, without hearing and touch we'd be hardpressed to perform them. That's because we use our secondary representational systems as a check—much the same way an archer uses the "thwack" of the arrow as it leaves the bow to confirm the visual sighting of a target. So, yes, primarily we come from one model of the world, but we never lose our supporting senses in the process. Kinesthetics are no different from visuals and auditories when it comes to cascading. **No one represents experience to herself solely in one sense.** While it's true that the visual will use her nimble sense of imaging a good deal of the time, and the auditory will rely primarily on her acuity of sound, we must always remember that visuals, auditories, and kinesthetics check their lead representations by scanning their other senses. That's why I call this cascading. We cascade from system to system in an effort to confirm what our primary or lead system has reported to us. And we demonstrate this by unconsciously moving our eyes to correspond with the specific representational system we're accessing at the moment. Have you ever conversed with someone and noticed her eyes moving here and there? Well, that's cascading. Have you ever spoken with anyone who stared down while talking with you, then looked up for no apparent reason? That's also cascading.

A good example of cascading is the way in which dominant visuals sometimes go to the upper left and right positions *after* they access an auditory or kinesthetic eye cue. This means they are first accessing a feeling about what you're saying (if they look to the lower right), then they see the picture (when they look to the upper left or right) with the feelings attached. For example, if you ask a visual if he was ever burned while cooking, the reply might well be "yes," while the person's eyes quickly dart down and right to the kinesthetic position—accessing the feeling of being burned—then to upper left to see a picture of himself being burned or a picture of his burned hand. Similarly, asking visuals about a favorite song or melody might bring their eyes to the level left position so they first hear the sounds or music, then to the upper right, where they see an image of the song's meaning with the sound attached.

Cascading.
Moving from representational system to representational

system. And demonstrating it through eye accessing cues.

One particularly advantageous result of knowing all this, is, of course, the ability to establish rapport. If we can ascertain how people are relating to us by watching not only their eye movements but the *order* in which they move their eyes as well, we can silently acquire their particular strategies. Now, I'm not going to ask you to digest the technology of creating rapport by unpacking someone's strategy right now. Strategy unpacking is carefully laid out for you in chapter 9. But I'm going to give you some insight into how to observe what others are thinking, literally by watching their eye movements.

The Silent Strategy

Now that we know the eyes reveal which representational system someone is relating through at any given time, it follows that knowing the *order* of these movements should spell out the process someone is using for her exact behavior at that moment. In fact, this turns out to be the case. To wit: if your boyfriend says to you, "I'd really like to see my friend Bob today. Do you think that would fit in with your plans? We could see each other later and take in a flick. Okay?" What you'd be getting *without* observing his eye accessing cues would only be language. But if you noticed the way his eyes moved, you'd be able to find out not only what representational systems he's cascading through but how to have rapport with him—even if you disagreed with the content portion of his idea. You see, since rapport is defined as offering behavior back with grace and elegance, replying with the same representational language and using the same *sequence* of representations as depicted by his eye cues will, in effect, create rapport. To illustrate:

"I'd like to **see** my friend Bob today." (Eyes UP and to the RIGHT meaning *visual constructed*.)

"Do you think that would **fit** in with your plans?" (Eyes DOWN and to the RIGHT, meaning *kinesthetic*.)

"We could **see** each other later and take in a **flick**." (Eyes UP and to the RIGHT, meaning *visual constructed*.)

Now you've got something to work with. You have targeted his representations not only through language but through his eye accessing cues as well. He's told you his exact strategy for being in rapport with him for the specific behavior called "what I would like to do this afternoon." Having this "formula" of rapport, though it's limited to afternoon activities, gives you a totally new and very effective tool of influence. With it, you may disagree with his plans—even alter them to your preference—without breaking rapport. You see, you'll be offering back to him his very own personal formula, which is visual constructed to kinesthetic to visual constructed, or: V →K →V.

What do you think will happen if you reply within the same representational context, meaning first visual, then kinesthetic, and then visually again? Do you think you'll be on the same wavelength? Do you think you'll be in rapport? *Absolutely*!

Now, if you have this supposedly wonderful condition of rapport, but disagree with what he wants to do, do you think this will break the rapport and possibly cause an argument? *Absolutely not*!

When you're in rapport, disagreeing with another's viewpoint is not only incidental, but can actually be utilized to change *their* point of view to *your* point of view.

This is obviously quite a sweeping statement. It's likely the most powerful concept in the technology of rapport and will be useful in ways that are probably not apparent to you at this moment. But even more important, this technology will allow you, maybe for the first time in your experience, to take charge of your life and actually produce results and outcomes that will create happiness, satisfaction, and contentment from day to day.

Though people's language may want for richness, eye accessing cues rarely lie. If your buddy says to you, "You know, I was really wild about her," and looks to the lower left, how do you think he's representing her to himself? Take a moment and think or refer to the eye accessing chart. If you said he was hearing her voice or something she told him, look to your left and experience the sound of applause. Though he never said a word, you knew what he was thinking because his looking to the lower left tells you he's hearing a familiar sound. Suppose, later on in the conversation, he says, "I remember the last time I was with her. It was unbelievable," and looks to the upper left? What's going on? You can lay odds he was seeing an image of her or the two of them together. Now, what if he says nothing—I mean *total* silence—but looks to the lower right? You can be certain he's gone directly from the image to a *feeling about* the image. In fact, ten bucks says his next words will be something about how he's feeling.

Let's take this even further.

Your buddy, in response to the question, "When's the last time you were with Annie?" looks to the left, then to the lower right, and then to upper left. What's he thinking?

1. Lower left: He **hears** her voice or a **sound** she makes.
2. Lower right: He **feels** something regarding that sound.
3. Upper left: He **sees** her or them together or apart.

What does all this eye movement tell you? *Tons.* It lets you know where your friend is, experientially, right now; it allows you to really know what he's thinking; it gives you wonderful insight into why he's behaving the way he is; *plus*, and this is possibly the most important of all, *it allows you to glide into his model of the world and be in rapport with him*—**instantly!**

Did you know that just by watching his eyes, you would be able to establish and maintain a deeper and more profound level of rapport while supporting him in what he's experiencing? Well, you can. Follow along. Suppose you said—(and notice how we keep our representations in the same order he keeps his):

"I know that just thinking of Annie is like **listening** to her. And I know she was always someone who could bring you in **touch** with your **feelings**; but **watching** the two of you together was incredibly natural, and I can **see** you think the same."

You've just succeeded in establishing a deep rapport with your friend. You see, first, you've spoken to him in his language. Second, you've pretty much described what he was thinking. Last, you've told him all this in the exact order in which he thought it. Now this last point is a big one. When we relate to people through their exact strategy or formula for a specific behavior, even if we don't know what the behavior is called, we can't help but be in rapport with them. You see, what we've done here is become exactly like our friend. We've become a mirror. We're thinking, talking, and acting exactly as he is. How could he avoid being in rapport with us? Is he going to reject his own language, thoughts, and behavior? No way. Remember, people like people who are like themselves.

This is where we are right now: we've learned to initiate rapport by speaking in the same representations as others, and in this chapter we've learned about eye accessing cues and the important role they play in defining people's subjective experience and what rapport is for them. Moreover, we've learned that these technologies, by their very nature, bring about rapport. Now we need to learn how to create rapport in such a way as to influence those whose trust and compliance we desire.

I want to lead you now to the realm of strategic rapport. But first we must learn another vital component of rapport establishment. It's the last crucial step we need to be aware of in nonverbal communication. In the following chapter, then, we will build on and enhance what we've learned so far, then move on to the art of strategies, where we really come face to face with the wizardry of instant rapport.

8

THE MIRRORING/MATCHING PROCESS

I T'S autumn. The leaves are turning crimson and bright yellow and the signs of evening are ushered in by spiral wisps of smoke from chimneys. It's the time of year that makes the countryside and mountains especially attractive. Late one chilly October evening, you decide to take in a movie with a friend. While waiting on the ticket line, you become involved in an interesting discussion with some other people. The topic heats up and pretty soon all are giving their points of view along with their evaluations. It so happens that you and your friend find yourselves on one side of a friendly debate, while the others try to find a weak point in your position. As the minutes pass you notice not only that you and your friend are winning, but that even though you've not rehearsed, the two of you are in perfect alignment. Those points your friend is responding to are very much complementary to what you've been putting across, and vice versa. As the moments pass, your friend begins to finish sentences that you've started. Part of you is conscious of this and very excited. A smile crosses your face. You're about to present the bottom line, which the last few minutes of debate have supported. You open your mouth to speak, and as the words come out you notice a pleasing harmony highlighting your voice. It's your friend, saying the exact same words you are!

Each and every one of us has had this experience. Sometimes it's with a friend, sometimes with an acquaintance. We've probably had the same experience with total strangers as well. We think, "How did he know what I was going to say?" or, "I thought she was going to say that, but how did I know?" Often, we chalk it off to synchronicity or random chance and leave it at that. However, I'll bet there are more than a few of you who wish you could re-create that experience of commonality or alignment with someone you're very much related to. Like your wife or boyfriend or boss, maybe? If so, you've come to the right place. Because what our friends have in common, what they're in alignment about, is, quite naturally, rapport.

What's that you say? How does rapport have anything to do with being on the same team or finishing someone else's thoughts? A lot. Without rapport, sharing a goal or a common purpose is a difficult task. Sort of like running in a marathon and not being in shape. With rapport, anything is possible between people. It's magic. Rapport is to relationships what fuel is to a car. Friendships without rapport are so mired in wasted energy that they shouldn't even be called friendships. I guess that's why we have the word *acquaintance*. When we're acquainted, we have a cursory knowledge. When we know, we have a conscious certainty.

When we think about those we know and esteem, we often admire how they look or how they think or talk or maybe even dress. It could be any quality(s) really, as long as we hold them within our experience as valued. Because of this high regard, we very naturally seek to incorporate some of these behaviors within ourselves. I think there's a whole long Freudian explanation for this, but the point is that we seek to be like, or to incorporate within us, those parts of others which we consider good and worthwhile. We want to be on the same wavelength—at least in a few ways. On the occasions when we're successful at doing this, we feel good. We feel a special closeness with them. We feel as if we know what they're thinking, what they like, and what pleases them. When this happens, sometimes we call, or want to call, these people friends. We admire them and feel an affinity toward them. We desire to be in harmony with them. Sometimes, we're actually able to create the condition of rapport.

I first noticed this in my own life years ago. In my sophomore year in college, I realized I was filled with awe for the professor who taught me my first year of organic chemistry. He was so smart and so incredibly knowledgeable about the subject, and had such a command of his area of specialty—molecular orbital theory—that it was inspiring to hear him lecture. Not that I was a terrific chemistry student. But by having this affinity for him, I realized that after a while, especially during lab, I was acting a little like him. I was developing his gestures, his tone of voice, even his habit of staring down at the floor while mulling over a problem. After about a month, I noticed that when I was in his class, I acted even more like him. And then a funny thing happened. When I would speak with him, one on one, I'd really understand the subject. Though I didn't know it at the time, I had been mirroring him very effectively, and quite unknowingly had built a powerful rapport with him.

The same thing happened with my girlfriend. At the beginning of our relationship there was a lot of physical attraction. And then came attraction of another sort. She was the picture of exactly what I wanted in a woman. She was articulate, extremely gracious and ladylike, and was someone I admired. She was very "there," almost lionhearted in her approach to people and life. One day it dawned on me that I was incredibly attracted to this stalwart manner of hers. It was so appealing. Well, before long I noticed that I began relating to people in a somewhat allied manner. I was talking and relating more and more like my girlfriend. The interesting thing was that it had a positive effect on our relationship. When I was with her I was becoming more and more like her, though she was never consciously aware of it. This was outstanding because it opened up new paths for us to explore. By and by, and as a result of my expanded class of behaviors, my girlfriend began acting more and more like me, and I began to experience her on a new and even more intimate level. We had reached a level of rapport that was really quite incredible. Yet, all the while, I didn't understand what was happening, nor did I even think about what it would be like to create this condition with anyone else. I was just thrilled to death that whatever it was, it was beautiful and it was mine. Though I left it alone for the longest time, somewhere in the back of my head was the fantasy of being able to have this kind of connection with anyone, at will, and not only in my personal life.

Mirroring creates this connection.

Mirroring is the simplest technology we have in our rapport arsenal. Yet, for all of its guilelessness, it remains a very quick and effective way to create rapport.

> **Mirroring is the technology whereby we offer back another's nonverbal behavior.**

The assumption rapport-technology makes is that by offering back to someone a mirror of her behavior, we become, in essence, just like her. If we include in our definition that people are most attracted to those like themselves, the result of mirroring should produce a state of rapport. And in fact we find this to be so.

When we mirror people, through matching their behavior, we're offering them not only visible and subconscious images of themselves, but images that are delivered without *our* meanings attached to them. In other words, people are seeing themselves without our *comments* about them. This frees them to drink in their personal likeness and connect their own unconscious meaning to it, as we all do. The nifty part of all this is that as we become more and more like the people we're mirroring, we build more rapport.

There are wonderful examples of mirroring all around, everywhere, and you already know a lot about it because, to some degree, it's something you already do. We mirror people and circumstances in the course of our lives so that we're appropriate and socially adept and poised. When we go to Broadway or to a movie or the ballet, don't we behave the way everyone else does in the audience? Don't we take our place in the theater, give our attention to the stage, even raise our head when everyone else does? I mean, you don't sit down and take off your clothes when the curtain goes up, do you? I hope not. (That would definitely be breaking rapport—especially with the people sitting closest to you!) You mirror the behavior of the audience and behave like them. Did you ever get the feeling, while in an audience, that all of you had a common purpose? Even that you felt a rapport with them? You know, as the lights go down and everyone hushes up and becomes still, waiting for the curtain to rise? You may have sensed that at the time, the people sitting next to you were in the exact same state as you, filled with anticipation and excitement, totally directed in their attention to the stage. At that single moment, you and they are in an almost total rapport. Even day-to-day problems you brought into the theater fade to black as the lights go down and you bring your consciousness and awareness to the stage, while mirroring everyone else. Yes, at that moment in time, you and the hundred or thousand people you're enjoined with are in rapport.

But mirroring doesn't have to be on such a large scale. Are we mirroring when we go to church? Absolutely. Next time you're there, look down the pew in which you're sitting and you'll notice that many in the congregation are postured the same way you are. We literally conform our body styles to others' while praying. How about the nights we're out with "the guys"? Do we talk with them the way we do at home? No way. We mirror their language content so that we're like them and are more comfortable for them to be with. Take a look at dancing, an obvious example of mirroring and leading. Do you recall what it was like when you fell into sync while gliding past the band? Dancing, in many ways, is a human caricature of our fundamental drive to be in synchrony with one another. Have you ever watched children at play? All they do is mirror. They watch their friends and try to do what they're doing. In fact, a large part of language acquisition in children is dependent on the process of mirroring. And when we relate with children, when we try to establish rapport with them, don't we automatically mirror their height by bending or stooping so that we're on eye level with them? You bet. Yet, because it is such a normal, day-to-day affair, the subliminal shadings of mirroring are barely noticed. What, then, could be a more effective technology to create rapport than something that already exists and works exceptionally well? *And* something that we are already masters of?

Mirroring works.

Remember when you were a kid and you and a friend would play the game "copy-cat"? You know, whatever your friend did, you did too? If he moved his right arm, you moved your right arm. If she smiled, you smiled. If she suddenly laughed, you did the same. You even tried to say what he was saying almost at the same time. Well, that's mirroring. And it works just about the same way now that you're an adult as it did when you were a child, except that it's just a little more refined. Let me share with you my first conscious experience with mirroring.

While studying an area of psychology called cognitive styles, I accidentally tripped upon an obscure paper on thought expression through nonverbal modalities. At the end of the paper, I noticed that the footnotes included a reference to mirroring and matching. Not understanding what that meant, I ignored it completely, until by fortuitous circumstances I had the good luck to gain access to a vast and revered psychological library. Within the first hour there, I found a manuscript on behavior modeling actually dog-eared on the title page. Not one to ignore this coincidence, I read it quickly—it wasn't a very long monograph—then borrowed it, took it home, and read it again.

It was almost too simple. There wasn't any complex jargon or stuff to memorize or superior mentality needed in order to use this apparently amazing tool. The bottom line was simply this: if you mirror—that is to say, act very much like another person, while in the company of that person—a state of rapport will materialize. And if you've done a good job of mirroring someone, it's possible to test for rapport by taking the lead. In other words, if you've truly established rapport, the person you've been mirroring will begin to mirror you when you take the lead. So, when you move your head up, the person you've achieved rapport with should follow your lead by moving his head up, too. Similarly, if you put your hand in your pocket, the other person should follow. And so on. Part of this sounded like complete and utter nonsense to me. But a voice inside said, "You've got to admit it, if it works, it could really be unbelievable." To be honest, the whole thing sort of fascinated me and I set about the task of learning mirroring so that I could try it out on some unsuspecting "victim." I had a whimsical attitude about it, though, not really accepting that such a thing was credible. But in any event, after modifying the technique and altering it for the sake of simplicity I had learned enough of it to try it out "on the road." I really had no idea how I would actually do this or what would happen if I succeeded, but I knew I just had to try. In point of fact, however, I essentially forgot about it until some weeks later, while I was having dinner with my good friend Becky, who happens to be the dean of theology at a very famous university.

Becky, a remarkably brilliant and talented minister, at the time was struggling valiantly, albeit somewhat unsuccessfully, to put the finishing touches on a pet community project, and she thought I might be of some assistance to her. We hadn't had dinner together in a few weeks, and hearing her voice on the phone was always a delight—she really has a way of communicating that's music to the ears. I forget at exactly what point I decided, but with some guilt and a lot of anticipation, I put my plan into action. Becky, tried and true and so heavenly forgiving, was to be my "victim."

We had a favorite bistro we frequented where we'd grab a bite and relax. But tonight it was going to serve an additional purpose. Tonight I was going to find out, with Becky's unwitting support, if the concept of mirroring was indeed a valid one or just so much "fluff."

Over a terrific dinner of northern Italian cuisine, we discussed and shared our points of view on just about everything. It was like that between Becky and me. She was terribly intuitive, and could place a feeling into a thought and then verbally express it in such a way that it was very "getatable." It was a challenge to keep up with her, but her sense of humor, which sometimes bordered on the outlandish, made the rest of her presentation really work. She was a lot of fun to be with. I guess you could say I had the perfect conditions for my little experiment.

The time came. We had finished our main course and were starting on the cappuccino when I plunged in. Initially, I started by mirroring her gross movements, like the way she was sitting. I crossed my legs, put my left elbow on the table and held my coffee cup in the same hand, up off the tablecloth. Next, I placed my head in the same position as hers, tilted slightly to one side. She always did that. That's when I remembered that mirroring is not a passive or static event. It's something you flow with over time. So when Becky put down her coffee cup, so did I. And when she shifted her weight from the back of the chair to a leaning-forward position, I followed in kind. Now as I was doing this, I kept in mind that one of the cardinal rules of mirroring is never to mimic. Let me give you that again:

> A cardinal rule of mirroring is never to mimic.

People have a built-in fail-safe alarm about someone's copying them movement for movement. And herein lies an important point. *When mirroring, slightly delay your pace, just for a brief moment or so, and don't use a direct playback of the observed behavior.* For instance, when Becky reached for her spoon to stir cream into her coffee, I *paused* for a quarter-second, then reached with my *opposite* hand for my spoon—but just moved it closer to me. And when she twirled a shock of her blond hair while considering a thought, as she often did, I used my opposite hand to straighten my collar. In essence, I was mirroring her with opposites. When we cross-mirror this way, our movements are not recorded with significance by another's consciousness, yet they *are* given meaning by the person's *un*conscious mind.

Try to be in rhythm as much as possible. For example, if someone has a particular meter in the way she speaks, see if you can match that pace. And if she breathes deeply or shallowly, mirror that, too. In fact, it's okay to mirror everything about another person, as long as we never violate the prime directive of noninterference: never mimic. It doesn't work anyway, and people's minds quickly "fix" on it, destroying whatever rapport you may have achieved up to that point. Well, Becky always took deep, deliberate breaths, so as much as I could, I did the same, either while I spoke to her or subtly, as she spoke to me.

Then an interesting thing happened. Long before I even started to look for signs of success, it dawned on me that Becky and I were having a particularly wonderful time and were truly delighting in each other's company. For a moment or two, I became so aware of this that I forgot what I was doing and automatically smiled her beaming smile back to her—literally mirroring her without being consciously aware of it! I knew then that we had reached rapport. But this wasn't how it was supposed to be. I mean, except for a subjective experience of being on the same wavelength and feeling very connected to her, how did I rationally know we were in rapport? Then I discovered the importance of leading, and how it is the acid test of rapport.

> Leading is generating behavior for another to mirror.

If you begin to lead, and the person you're with follows, you have a black-and-white, rational, and objective test for rapport. Interestingly, I was having such a lovely time with Becky, that I almost abandoned my experiment. But I persisted, quieting the part of me arguing for an easy evening without any effort. Then again, I thought, I wasn't really making much of an effort at what I was doing anyway, so why not forge ahead and see what happens?

It was while we were talking about family and how she missed her sister back home in Wyoming that I changed the pace and took the lead. I expected that some unbelievable thing would happen, but nothing did. I didn't really know what I was hoping for, except maybe that Becky would start to do what I was doing. Then I remembered I hadn't *done* anything yet. So I reached out with my left arm for the sugar and placed it next to my empty coffee cup. Without missing a beat, and not bothering to stop talking, Becky reached for the cream and placed it next to her coffee cup! Well, you know those cartoon characters who see something they can't believe? You know how their eyes fly out of their heads? That's exactly how I felt! I was just astonished! But pressing on through the amazement, I next uncrossed my legs, then recrossed them in the opposite direction. Again, with just a few seconds' pause, Becky moved her chair slightly away from the table, uncrossed her legs, then recrossed them in the opposite direction! At this juncture I was so mesmerized—I guess *shocked* is a better word—that I couldn't believe what was happening! "This is unreal! How could it be!?" I stuttered to myself. Stopping my thoughts momentarily, I wiped my forehead; Becky followed by scratching the bridge of her nose. Then I took a drink of water, and Becky followed by lifting her coffee cup for a sip. But she didn't even have any coffee in it! And I swear, she looked like she didn't even notice it! We were so in rapport that whatever I did, her unconscious mind interpreted as something *she* should do because, in point of fact, I was being like her. I was acting the way Becky was comfortable acting. How could she not want to behave like herself? It was then that I got incredibly clear about the power of mirroring and the creation of rapport. They were joined almost cosmically, one entwined with the other, as naturally as hydrogen and oxygen molecules are in water.

It was an especially wonderful evening and it lingered for some hours until the owner tactfully reminded me it was closing time. I remember looking at Becky with such empathy that when I leaned near to kiss her, she automatically met me halfway, almost as if we were following an especially well-written script. It was, in a word, wonderful.

But I wanted to see how far I could go before breaking rapport. It wasn't what I really felt like doing, but it was important for me to ascertain what limits, if any, there were on mirroring. I quickly found out. As the check came and went, I measurably turned up the pace on my lead, literally following one gesture with another. This produced the effect you would see watching a video jammed in the fast-forward mode. There was Becky, hands and legs flying as if inadvertently stuck in an electric socket. For a moment I thought we were trapped inside a Daffy Duck cartoon. This lasted for about ten or fifteen seconds, until I reached the point I call "critical rapport." At this threshold, you approach a speed at which rapport is broken by the mind's inability to process its mirror image. What happens is not only a break in rapport but the introduction of annoyance. In fact, as I crashed through the rapport barrier, Becky suddenly stopped moving with me and looked straight into my eyes with a puzzled expression. "What are you doing, Michael?" she snapped. There was no doubt about it, she was definitely annoyed; as if something had been bothering her for the last few minutes but she didn't know precisely what it was. People usually don't know *why* they're annoyed at this point, but it seems that "speeding" collapses a fresh rapport quite effectively. Becky did have a sense, though, of what was bothering her. Her mind was telling her that in some way I was the cause of the irritation. What had been a most lovely evening was now shattered by my foolish and inarticulate bumbling. I never forgot this. If you play with someone's trust while actively mirroring them, you run a pretty good risk of ruining the friendship or whatever rapport you have at the time.

Over the next week, Becky and I met twice, at which times I immediately and gratefully reestablished rapport. I explained all about mirroring and my research in rapport-technology, with which she already knew I was heavily involved. We did reconnect eventually and to this day enjoy a truly close friendship.

You can mirror and match practically any portion of someone's behavior. To guide you and give you a point of reference to be creative from, the following material describes the best general areas of behavior to mirror. I encourage you to be resourceful in devising new parameters to work with.

Body Movements

When you mirror people's body movements, you're mirroring the way they walk, sit, use their hands, gesture, hold themselves, and any other physical manifestations of nonverbal communication.

The way you mirror should always be subtle and fluid. It's hardly ever necessary to make sudden, sharp movements in an attempt to duplicate someone's behavior. And for a majority of the time, direct copying should be avoided. A good strategy to use is cross-mirroring. That's where you use opposite gestures to match behavior. For instance, if someone adjusts his tie, you can smooth your collar. If she's tapping her finger on the table, you can quietly tap your foot on the floor. What would you do if someone played with his ring? Well, it might be a good idea to adjust your wristwatch band. Suppose someone constantly shifted her weight from foot to foot while talking with you. Leaning toward her, then away, may be a good way to effect the mirror. The point is, you want the message to reach people's unconscious minds, where it will be interpreted as a likeness of themselves. If you're stiff and very direct, you'll attract their consciousness, and you might hear, "What are you doing?" or, "Do you have a problem?"

Voice

This is probably one of the best ways to mirror someone. Since almost half of the total communication package
is delivered through voice tone, mirroring this portion of
behavior is very effective.

From time to time, people who have taken my seminars
call me and want to communicate something to me. This
is always challenging because I speak with people from all
over the country, and I'm always searching for ways to make
them more comfortable on the phone. One of the ways I do
this is to become aware of the particular dialect or regional-
ism in their voice, and then mirror it. Being an auditory, it's
not that hard for me to pick up the subtle differences in
people's accents. This is something you can do right off the
bat because people like it when you talk the way they do,
because we generally speak at the same pace as we prefer to
listen. Even if they're consciously aware that you're, let's
say, in the West but are talking with a Southern accent, it
really makes them comfortable. I especially enjoy talking
with Southerners because I'm able to mirror their rolling
inflections quite well and immediately form a good rapport,
even over the phone. Remember, the only person who may
be uneasy with it is you. Just imagine calling New York
from Texas and hearing someone whose voice sounds familiar; a voice that reminds you of home. Wouldn't it make the
conversation easier and therefore more productive?

Voice mirroring consists not only of accent but of tone,
timbre, inflection, tempo, cadence, and intonation. Mirroring
these can be quite effective. If someone has a soft tone to his
voice, mirror that with a soft tone. If she speaks slowly,
match her speed. Have you ever had a disagreement with
someone and tried to overpower him by talking louder?
That's the same thing as being in a foreign country and
yelling at someone who speaks a different language in an
effort to get him to understand. It's idiotic. Have you ever

been in a quiet, intimate restaurant with your lover and whispered something tender in her ear, only to have her totally break rapport by replying in a full-bodied voice? I know someone who is so good at vocal mirroring that he can be in rapport with someone without speaking that person's language at all. He simply matches the vocal signature of the particular language as well as that of the person he's talking to. It's unbelievable to witness. Look, it isn't necessary to be a professional to get the results you want. But I think you'll be surprised at how just attempting to match vocal nuances will increase the ease of high rapport.

Facial Expressions

We all have certain expressions that we feel comfortable with. Sometimes these are subtle creases at the mouth or corners of the eyes, and at other times they're very obvious expressions such as a particular way of smiling or frowning. We all know people who have a habit of winking when they want to drive home a point, right? We've all seen the masterful way Johnny Carson uses this simple gesture to make a guest feel secure. Do you think Carson would respond to that same gesture if used elegantly? Of course. Gracefully mirroring these kinds of expressions will definitely enhance the probability of rapport.

Specific Gestures

These are a favorite of mine. People have their own repertoire of personalized gestures that are easy to mirror because they are unique. Sometimes it's as simple as moving your hand in the same direction as that of the person you're with; other times, it could be tapping on the table in the same rhythm as the respiration of whomever you're with. When people are conversationally engaged in making a point, they tend to use their bodies in specific ways to give added meaning and impact to what they're communicating. I like to cross-mirror them by using my body in the same way, but perhaps in the opposite direction or at a different angle.

Breathing

Matching the breathing patterns of others is an excellent way of forming rapport. I'm not being esoteric here. And I don't mean that to achieve connection you have to be in complete sync to the point where you pass out. Simply mirror, as closely as you can, the depth, frequency, and amplitude of your partner's respiration. I do this all the time with my friends nowadays because they're always expecting me to mirror them in the same old obvious ways. I try to explain that rapport-technology isn't something secretive; it's just another way of encouraging good communication. Of course, I'm mirroring their breathing as I say this.

Once you are familiar with the different parameters of mirroring you begin to lead. Leading is generating behavior for another to mirror, and it's the process by which we verify the establishment of rapport. This is accomplished by changing the pace of mirroring and observing if our partner matches our behavior.

After I mirrored Becky for a few minutes, I checked to see if she had reached rapport by leading her. I simply took the "lead" and noticed whether she did what I did. The first time you lead successfully will really be an eye-opener. The best way I can describe it is to compare it to horseback riding. When you learn to ride, a lot of what you do is listen to instruction and canter around a large corral until the trainer is satisfied with your performance. But the most thrilling part of riding is when you're out on your own on some mountain trail, and you become one with your horse. The connection and empathy you develop with your animal as he naturally follows your lead by mirroring your movements, is akin to the way you lead your partner when you verify for rapport. When another responds to your lead by mirroring *your* behavior, the feelings that it generates in you are overwhelming. Not only does it validate your skills as a rapport-rich communicator, but the alignment and grace that are discovered are like nothing you've ever experienced before.

You want to be easy and gentle when you begin leading. In fact, if you're not temperate and open, you'll find leading quite frustrating. You have to remember that you're looking to verify a state of rapport, and that implicit in this process is an attitude of serenity and sureness. Also keep in mind that when people take your lead, they're trusting you, for however long, with the very core of who they are. Don't startle them by suddenly being shocked at your success; and don't laugh and be inappropriate about the power you've acquired. If you muff it here, often you won't get a second chance. I had beginner's luck with Becky. However, I came awfully close to losing a friend.

If you've tried to lead but have elicited no response, you're not in rapport yet. That's okay. Don't be discouraged. Try again. Sometimes it'll take you fifteen or twenty seconds to gain a successful lead. Other times it may take four or five minutes. It depends on what's going on at the time relative to both of you. You'll find that sometimes it is easier to effect a good lead than at other times. This is to be expected. As you polish your rapport skills and become more and more graceful in their use, not only leading but rapport itself will become easier to bring about.

Once you have begun leading, the time has come to use other skills of rapport, such as anchoring (which you're going to master in chapter 10), strategy playback, and rapport linguistics. However, one technology doesn't necessarily precede the other. The beauty of instant rapport is that you can be as creative as your heart desires. Ultimately, you will find your best style and favorite techniques, with which you'll feel the most comfortable and achieve the most success.

A word about "body language": it implies that there is meaning behind someone's behavior. This may or may not be so, but it's not what we're talking about here. In mirroring, we seek to match another's behavior, not to understand it. Other than specific gestural accessing cues, the information we deduce from people's use of their arms or legs can be very misleading. If, for example, a woman crosses her legs while talking with us, does this mean she is being seductive or that her leg muscles are fatigued? If your husband or boss crosses his arms, does it mean he's closed to what you're saying or that he's chilly? For our purposes, this information is not only extraneous but can be misleading. We establish rapport on a need-to-know basis. Since body language can misinform us because it's arbitrary, we don't need to learn about it. Mirroring is about being in step with someone, not about what their steps mean.

One last caveat about mimicking. In our society, we have a very strong cultural bias against being mimicked. Very simple, people don't find being mimicked complimentary. Indeed, it's not only frowned upon but is often interpreted as rude. If rapport is what you're after, mimicking is something you should actively avoid. I mention this because of the inevitable temptation we have, while mirroring, to copy someone's exact behavior. Sometimes you'll find it's appropriate to do that. But for the majority of the time, mirroring should avoid exact duplication of behavior, relying for the most part on the natural ability we all share to use our graceful and artistic selves; that part of us which is the stuff rapport is made of.

Okay, its time. Earlier we talked about the language of rapport. Then we moved on to the magic of eye accessing cues and saw how they give us entrée to someone's thoughts. In this chapter we departed from those observable technologies and got involved in the creation of rapport through mirroring. Now, to achieve an even deeper level of connection, and create a total—and even more profound—rapport we will learn how to unpack someone's strategy.

9

THE STRATEGIES

DEFINITION OF THE MIND: The mind is a stack of representations. It is a multisensory linear arrangement of total records of successive moments of now.

THIS chapter's a killer. It opens up a whole new world of technology that will leave you entranced, enlightened, and fearsomely empowered. You will actually be equipped with what is probably the most potent technology in our rapport arsenal. For some of you, this will be the first time that learning a technology will be not only useful but used. It will also be a natural step in the direction of more effective and complete relationships. You will find, within the following pages, an incredible new methodology that will create change in yourself and in those with whom you communicate. It is here that we probe the deepest on our journey to instant rapport.

Sometimes rapport is available to us spontaneously through random chance, and that's good when you want to have rapport. But sometimes we get stuck in rapport when it's *not* advantageous. Like the time you unwittingly caused the doorman to involve you in a conversational rapport while running upstairs in the hope of being *only* an hour late for dinner. Remember how hard it was to break away from him? How about the time your doctor paraded before you his newborn's picture, complete with commentary, instead of giving you the results of your laboratory tests. Remember how you wanted to rip the report out of his hands but just smiled, and gushed your heartfelt wonder at the photograph?

Unfortunately, a good many of us endure rapportless lives totally at the effect of random rapport, such as when we've tried, unsuccessfully, to enroll the boss in a particular cause. Or when rapport has absolutely eluded us, such as the times we just couldn't get along with someone we really wanted to like or to have like us. Being at the effect of random rapport can be as bad as not being able to create it to begin with.

Why Learn About Strategies?

Strategies provide a set of tracks, if not an historical tour, across the landscape of the mind, and are probably the most effective tool we have to create an ordered rapport; thereby, entering someone's model of the world and sharing it with him. Since we have a strategy for just about everything we do, it's important to understand their function and how people arrive at a particular set of strategy components. Knowing this, and following the most basic axiom of rapport—*people like people who are like themselves*—we can "mirror" their strategy and so become exactly like them.

What precisely do I mean by strategy, anyway? Probably, for most of us, a strategy is something a general in the army might use in fighting battles, or what a football team uses to outfox the opposition. We even hear the word in business meetings, usually referring to a number of actions a company may use to accomplish specific goals. Any specific behavior involves its own strategy for fulfillment. One of my favorite examples of this is the moviemaking strategy of Woody Allen. All of us would probably agree that he's highly kinesthetic. Yet, his strategy for moviemaking is strongly auditory. The sounds of words are everything in his movies. Not only what they mean, but how they're said—especially their rhythm. In fact, he counts heavily on words to produce specific feelings. One has only to observe his use of narration as a deus ex machina for so many of his works. My favorite example of this is the brilliant movie *Annie Hall*. Woody actually opens it with a direct aside to the audience. This opening soliloquy, if you will, is so rare in moviemaking that one can hardly discount its auditory implications. Once the words he produces for a scene lead to feelings, then he creates the visual representations we see on the screen. His strategy for making movies is clearly A →K →V, that is to say:

> auditory representation leads to a
> kinesthetic representation which leads to a
> visual representation.

Since his strategy's first component is auditory, we'd loosely refer to it as an auditory moviemaking strategy.

In my early twenties, my friends and I would cruise the college scene in Manhattan and plan a strategy for meeting women. Sometimes these strategies weren't so successful. In fact, while the planning was terrific fun, the execution was too often met with laughter and ridicule. But as time passed, we continually refined our socializing strategies, and some of us developed quite an array of them, eventually settling on the few that consistently worked. Of course, I didn't realize it then, but I was learning about rapport and how we specifically create it.

In rapport-technology, a strategy is *a particular sequence of representations that, when followed, produces a specific behavior or outcome leading to rapport.*

In part I, we discussed three different, distinct ways in which all of us "represent" experience. We learned that some people represent experience primarily through what they see; some through what they hear; others, through how they feel. We've categorized them as being either visual, auditory, or kinesthetic—that, in general, they *lead* with one of these senses or representational systems. We also talked about how people could be, let's say, highly visual, yet use their sense of hearing or touch to complete specific tasks. This is a belief that we should fully understand; it works for us to accept it as another of our rules of rapport:

We are *primarily* either visual, auditory, or kinesthetic. However, for many of our behavioral strategies, we *sometimes* lead with a representational system *other* than our primary one.

Now I don't mean that if, for example, we are primarily visual—see the world through pictures or images—that we *must* have an auditory or kinesthetic strategy for something. That's just not true. However, because we all develop as unique individuals and some of our senses get more developed than others—*in specific areas*—we sometimes lead with one of our other senses for specific strategies. In fact, we put together strategies for almost everything we do. We have strategies for:

> motivation
> buying
> selling
> love
> attraction
> communicating
> sex
> making money
> independence and dependence
> friendships

and hundreds more. One strategy for nearly everything we're involved with. This is really nifty when we consider that by ascertaining a person's strategy for, let's say, falling in love, we can actually bring her to reexperience that feeling, but within the context of *ourselves*. So if you happen to be playing back someone's love strategy, guess what? Your chances of that person falling in love with you, all other conditions being equal, are magnified a thousand percent. White magic? Absolutely! And strategy rapport is virtually unlimited. It can be applied to *any* strategy. You will be able to ascertain—or what I call "unpack"—someone's strategy for almost anything and thereby create rapport within the framework of that strategy. So if you're selling dresses, or computers and software programs, or encouraging someone to be motivated, or you want to sell your services, just unpack your client's strategy for buying and you'll have an instant rapport within that framework. Having rapport with those you do business with will automatically and visibly improve your earning capacity. Remember, rapport is the condition where you offer back people's behavior and fulfill the first rule of rapport: *people like people who are like themselves.*

Strategies are uncannily similar to other things that require a specific ordered sequence of events for them to work properly. Examples that come to mind are bicycle riding, negotiating, learning the multiplication tables, deal closing, calling someone on the telephone, cooking an omelet, and driving a car. They all require you to follow a very specific chain of events. The beauty of strategies is that they always work if you remain true to their exact blueprint. Let's pick one of the examples above and illustrate how a strategy looks, while also discussing the simple concept of syntax or order.

All of us, during the course of a day, use the telephone. In fact, we use it so often that we never think about how to use it. We just pick up the receiver and dial. But stop right there. When we want to call someone, do we dial any old number? Do we just randomly push buttons and hope for the best? Of course not. If we tried to communicate like that, no one would ever hear us. Yet, some people use exactly that strategy for most of what they do, and then they wonder why they aren't understood. The *numbers* we dial and the *order* in which we dial them will give us many different outcomes. To reach a particular person in a particular location, we must be very specific about the *syntax*, or order, in which we dial. Having the right numbers is an excellent start, but without the correct syntax (order) we won't ever connect. And the area code must be correct. If just one bit of information is not in syntax, you may dial the phone, but you'll get an outcome different from the one you want. Also, a particular outcome may have several different dialing strategies, as when the party we want has more than one phone number. So, right off the bat, you can see that strategies rely heavily on syntax and *specificity*. Without being specific, strategy unpacking is pointless. It's like driving to your friends' farmhouse in the country using a map without routes or addresses, maybe just an arrow or two as the only means of navigation. Trying to get there would be an exercise in futility. Gotta have the specifics. If you're not specific about syntax, that last sentence:

Gotta have the specifics
would *not* give you the outcome you want. As in:
The have specifics gotta

Of course there will always be some people who don't need the specifics. We all have people like that in our lives. They manage to produce an outcome; it's just not the one they wanted. Or they once produced a successful outcome by chancing upon the right strategy, say, for making money, but apply it to everything else in their lives as well. They can either only make money in a specific way in a specific situation, or they do everything in life as if it were a business proposition.

The importance of syntax can also be illustrated in the way a baker makes a cake. It's not only the ingredients that count, but the temperature of the oven and the time it takes to cook. That's all you need to know, right? Not totally. Again, remember our friend syntax. If you mix things in the wrong order (syntax), the cake won't come out the way you want—i.e., your outcome will be incongruent with your intention.

Ever made scrambled eggs? Well, try adding the butter *after* the eggs are scrambled (wimpy syntax). Or scrambling those eggs in perfect order, but at 700°F. for two hours. How about putting salad dressing on vegetables before they're harvested (wimpy syntax again). Get the point? When we endeavor to unravel someone's strategy, syntax is crucial. Yet, syntax is a graceful thing and will work for you time and time again as you become more adept and elegant in its use.

The Strategy: What It Is and How It Works

One of my best friends, a lovely woman who is the founder of her own successful company, met a terrific guy, stumbled upon his strategy for being attracted and falling in love, and had a wonderful rapport-rich relationship with him for quite some time. She really tapped in to this man's love strategy. By and by, the two grew apart and eventually became rapportless and hence out of love.

Now my friend, being a pretty resourceful woman, set about the task of keeping her life on track by doing what she always did: using those behaviors that worked for her and discarding those that didn't. However, she couldn't get her love life together. No matter what interest she expressed in a man, she never got a satisfactory response. Before long she grew quite upset about this.

"Ever since Barry left, I just can't seem to attract a man," she explained to me one night over dinner. "I mean, it's not that they don't find me appealing, it's just that after an initial meeting, or for sure by the end of the first date, that's it. I never see them again. They don't call. And on the occasions when I've called them, they were...well...they didn't seem very interested. Now at first, I hardly noticed this. I guess I was still feeling hurt and missing Barry. But as the months dragged on, I started to see a pattern. One date and I'd hear, 'Have a nice life.' Michael, I'm just so frustrated and upset. I don't know what I'm doing wrong, if anything, and I'm really at a loss."

The misty look in her eyes and the way she was accessing her constructed pictures, then checking them with her feelings, validated her statements. She was indeed stuck in an old behavior that obviously wasn't working for her.

"Tell me, Jennifer," I said, "what exactly do you do when you're out with a new guy? How do you relate? Is it very hard for you? Do you behave differently now than you did with Barry?"

"It's really not terribly hard for me now, Michael," she said. "It's been some time, you know, since Barry and I split up, and I try to relate to someone new as instinctively and up-front as I can. In fact, if anything, I behave toward them as genuinely and as interested as I did the first time I met Barry. So it's not as though I'm using some strange or different approach...."

Jennifer went on for a few more seconds, but I really didn't hear her. I had gotten all the information I needed, and I was struck by the obvious simplicity of the solution. The next thing I knew, I felt her touch my arm.

"Michael, you haven't heard a word I said. I can't believe you. I'm pouring my heart out and you're sitting there with this dumb grin on your face, not even listening!"

"I'm grinning, my friend, because I have the answer to

your problem!" I said. "What's driving these men away is your attraction strategy. You're still using the same old one. I mean, you're still using Barry's strategy for being attracted to you. Tell me, when you're out on a date, if you're attracted to one of these fellows, do you relate to him as you did with Barry?"

"Well, of course not. I could never do that."

"I mean, Jenny, do you talk and act with them pretty much the way you did on your first few dates with Barry?"

"If you mean, am I being myself, the answer is yes."

"Well, I can tell you, without question, that what you consider 'being yourself,' is being yourself the way you were with Barry. And given that, it's really no wonder you're not getting the responses you want. Though in a sense, Jenny, you *are* getting the responses you want. You're running Barry's attraction strategy because it worked for you once a long time ago. You stumbled on it when you first met him, as lovers often do, and you're still running it—though he's long gone. What I'm telling you now is that it's okay to let go of that strategy. I'm going to show you how to find out attraction strategies of other men, and after I do, I'm going to turn you loose on the world and hope you don't become the Pied Piper."

When I showed her how to find out someone's strategy for being attracted and falling in love, Jennifer was amazed to see how easy it was. I mean, she was wide-eyed and buzzing. In no time she became masterful at strategy unpacking and playback. At last report she was seen somewhere in Dallas mowing them down. Everyone she met fell in love with her. I narrowly escaped with my life.

Now, what did I tell her? What did I let her know that created such self-confidence and power within her? Nothing more than an explanation of strategies. Like a lot of wonderful things in life, strategies are simple, obvious, and powerful.

The key to successful rapport, naturally, is pinpointing someone's strategy for a particular behavior, such as attraction, and using that strategy when we relate with that person. So that if we want someone to be attracted to us, for example, we'd communicate with him using *his* strategy for attraction. If we wanted a person to buy something from us, we'd communicate with him using *his* strategy for buying. When this is executed properly, people very quickly fall into rapport with us; but even more relevantly, they fall into the *specific* **kind** *of rapport* that a particular strategy engenders.

Exactly how do we find out someone's strategy for a specific behavior; for instance, someone's love strategy? Do we just walk right up and say, "Hey, Charlie, tell me, what's your strategy for, ah, falling in love, or for ...oh...terrific sex?" Well, we could do that. But it's probably not the most elegant way to establish rapport. There is, fortunately, a more graceful and terribly effective model for unpacking a person's strategy.

Strategy Unpacking and Strategy Playbacks

Strategy Unpacking

What we do in unpacking someone's strategy is to get the person to slow down and replay for us some behavior we'd like to unravel, and then play it back to him to induce rapport. Kind of a "slo-mo instant replay." The way we bring people to do this is by asking certain specific questions about the strategy we're interested in discovering. These questions are designed so that people will express themselves through their sensory representational systems; in other words, in terms of images (visual), words and sounds (auditory), and feelings or touch (kinesthesia). Let me give you an example of what I'm talking about.

If you're in the real estate business, and want to sell Mr. Smith a particular property, you'll want to find out his strategy for buying real estate. Remember, buying real estate is just like any other behavior—no different in form from taking a shower or selling stationery. Everything we do in life can be broken down and fitted into one strategy or another. A strategy is like a formula, giving its observer a simple way to understand something that's complicated. In developing rapport, knowing someone's strategy for doing something is like having a very specific map of that person's internal wiring. If we follow the map's directions, it will lead us directly to rapport for a specific situation. So if we follow someone's "map" for eating, let's say, we'd be able to be in rapport with her within the context of eating. In other words, we'd always be able to make meals terrific for that person by knowing her map or strategy for great and satisfying meals. (Offhand, I know at least ten people who could benefit from knowing their lovers' eating strategies. But that's another story.)

If you know Mr. Smith's exact strategy for buying real estate, the result will be akin to knowing the correct numbers of a combination lock. Follow the right sequence, using the right numbers, and the safe opens. Well, if you know Smith's strategy for buying real estate, you've all but closed a deal. You see, armed with this knowledge, you create a powerful "real estate buying rapport" with him that will be virtually irresistible. Trust me on this, for just a while longer.

We're now going to ask a series of specifically designed questions to elicit sensory-based answers. By no means must your questions be as "bald" as the ones I've written. Think of the following questions as models that you can modify to be appropriate to the situation and to the level of familiarity.

The first question you ask him in your effort to unpack his real estate buying strategy will elicit the strategy's first step.

1. Can you tell me about a time when you bought real estate and were totally satisfied and delighted?

What you are doing here is bringing the person back to a time when he experienced having rapport within a certain context. In this case, it's buying real estate. Mr. Smith will, by a process known as transderivational search, go back into his memory to locate a specific experience in his life when the purchase of a piece of real property gave him a winning outcome. Maybe it was a time he enjoyed living in a particular house, or maybe it was the great deal he made on that house—it really doesn't matter. What counts is getting him to go back and step into an experience of being satisfied and delighted about buying a piece of property. He will do this by one of three familiar ways:

A visual process

An auditory process

A kinesthetic process

No matter which avenue he takes, though, he will assuredly complete his psychological search when he recalls a pleasant real estate buying experience. He'll let us know when he has this recollection very easily and very obviously—and in more than one way. First, he will verbally tell you about it. *Believe it or not, this isn't very important.* We're not really interested in Smith's "soap opera" or "script copy." Where we really want him to come from is his senses. We want him to relate his past satisfying experience through language that is "sensory descriptive." Specifically, through his senses of vision, hearing, and feeling.

Second, he will let you know when his search is complete by signaling with his physiology. You will observe him go "into state" when he's arrived.

A person is "in state" *when he physically exhibits or manifests his internal experience.*

If you've ever asked anyone about a terrific birthday present, or a wild love affair, or the death of a parent, you will easily see him go into state. His body may shift, his color changes, his eye expressions change—even his breathing will be altered. Sometimes this will be very obvious, as when a smile crosses the face or a tear drifts down the cheek; at other times it may be as subtle as a shoulder shrug or a shift in posture. When we recall any significant past experience, we go into state. Our job as rapport initiators is to notice these changes and use them as cues to help us in strategy unpacking.

You've posed the question: Can you tell me about a time when you bought real estate and were totally satisfied and delighted?

Smith will most likely respond with a particular experience he'll recall and represent to himself internally. He might say, "Yeah, sure, I remember. It was the house I bought with my wife and kids."

When he lets you know he's recalling an experience, verbally or nonverbally or both, you're ready for question 2.

2. Mr. Smith, can you tell me the very *first* thing that made you want to buy that particular piece of real estate?

1. Something you *saw*? Or was it
2. Something you *heard*? Or
3. Something that *touched* you or that you *felt*?

By asking him to be sensory-specific, Smith's reply will literally hand you the first step in his real estate buying strategy.

"Hmmm. I know this **sounds** funny," he says, "but I think the very first thing that **rang** true for me about that place was probably the way it just **sounded** so full of life. From the moment you walked in, you could **hear** the trees **rustling** in the afternoon **breeze** and the birds **chirping** away on the branches. It took me right back to my home as a child. Yeah, that was the very first thing I liked about the place."

Ta-da! You now have Smith's *first step* in his buying strategy. It is sound or hearing. When he recalls buying real estate successfully, the very first criterion he uses for a sense of satisfaction and delight is sound. He first needs to *hear* if it's the real estate he's going to purchase. As rapport builders, we naturally call this first step *auditory*, which we'll represent with the letter A.

Terrific! Now, on to the third step.

3. Mr. Smith, after you heard the breeze and the birds chirping, what was the *very next thing* you remember that satisfied and delighted you about that property?

1. Something you *saw*? Or was it
2. Something *else* you *heard*? Or
3. Something that *touched* you or that you *felt*?
Again, you've asked him to be sensory-specific.
"You mean after the sounds of outdoors?" he replies.
"Yes, sir. The very next thing."

"Hmmmm. I really can't . . . ah, yes, it was—it was the **feeling** I got from hearing those things. Like I told you, it reminded me of my home as a boy. What a **secure feeling** that was, y'know. A terrific **sense** of **togetherness**. Not like today at all."

Smith has just supplied us with strategy component number 2. The sounds of the outdoors lead to a *feeling*. A lovely feeling from his childhood. Let's represent feeling or touch with the letter K for *kinesthesia*. So far, then, we have:

A→K.

The next step is simply a repetition of the first two. We just plug in the information he supplies to us in the appropriate blanks, and feed him another sensory-based question.

4. Mr. Smith, after you *heard the breezes* and *the birds chirping*, which gave you *a feeling of security* and *togetherness*, what was the very next thing you remember that satisfied and delighted you about that place?

1. Something you *saw*? Or was it
2. Something else you *heard*? Or
3. Something else that *touched* you or that you *felt*?

"It's interesting you're asking me about all this," he says, "because it's been quite some time since I've **seen** the old place."

Now right here you have the information you've asked for. He's looking to the upper left to access remembered pictures and he's talking in visual processors ("... quite some time since I've **seen** the old place"). But even without knowing this, if you just let him continue, most times he'll supply you with everything you need to know. Your job is to observe and to listen.

"You know, I haven't really **seen** a **sunset** as **pretty** as those that **shone** through the living room of that place in quite a while. It was really somethin'."

Of course, Smith's third (and for us, final) strategy component is visual. Let's use a V to represent *visuality*. Now when we write down the three steps of Mr. Smith's real estate buying strategy, it looks like this: A→K→V.

This little gem of a formula is pure magic. It is, quite literally, the combination that will unlock the vault to Smith's exact method for buying real estate.

Technically, strategies can have almost endless numbers

of components to them. However, for the establishment of rapport, three steps or representations, such as Smith's, are really quite sufficient.

Keep in mind, though, that this formula is strictly limited to Mr. Smith's real estate buying strategy. This is *not* a general strategy. Although it is possible to meet someone who has the same real estate buying strategy as Smith's, it's rather unlikely. Remember that people are wired up uniquely, just like a combination lock or a telephone number. If just one representation is wrong or not in the right order, you won't get the result or the response you want.

"Now that I know Mr. Smith's exact real estate buying strategy," you might be wondering, "what am I going to do with it?" I'm glad you asked. What I'm about to show you will transform your experience of being in rapport with people forever.

If you remember, part of our definition of rapport was *to offer back with grace and elegance.* Well, if we offer back Smith's behavior, specifically his particular behavior of buying real estate, we will be in rapport with him. And, as we know, when you're in rapport with someone, achieving the outcome you want is a thousand percent more likely than when you have a rapportless condition. Let's offer back to Smith the real estate cake of his dreams: his unique strategy for buying real estate.

But wait! How, exactly, do we do this? Do we tell him to hear a breeze and feel secure, and then shove a contract under his nose? Of course not. Although judging from some of the ways I've seen real estate being sold, this would actually be an improvement.

Strategy Playback

As children, we loved having our parents tell us stories. It really didn't matter if they read them or recited them, or even if they were true, as long as they held our attention and kept us entertained. We didn't mind hearing these stories, did we? Even when we knew, after hearing them so many times, what the endings would be, the "stuff" of the stories—the content—was interesting. Though we knew in advance that Captain Hook was going to get his just rewards, it was still great fun hearing the drama unfold. Sometimes, due either to our parents' memory or lack of it, the characters would change and even some of the actual drama would get altered. But as long as the *gist* of the story remained intact, we came away with the same sense of satisfaction and delight as we had so many times before. For our parents, it was important that the stories they related had at least some implied or subliminal message. Sometimes it was a message about telling the truth, as in *Pinocchio*; sometimes about good and evil, as in *Peter Pan*; or about subtler things, as in the story of *The Fox and the Grapes*. Our parents were concerned about our getting the right message, and they took any opening they found to instill in us their concept of good or goodness. What our parents didn't know was that by using our own childish strategies, they could have gotten us to do much more than just learn the differences between good and bad, right and wrong, and the distinctions between Grumpy and Sneezy.

Psychologists have long known that the story is a powerful tool for creating change in people. Everyone tells stories. We have to. It's through storytelling that we're able to communicate something we feel is too sensitive to say directly. We use stories in place of overt language to communicate certain messages. We do this all the time but just aren't aware of it. You know those times when instead of explaining exactly what you mean, you'll say, "I once knew this person..." or "A long time ago..." or "I once heard about this fellow..." and then continue with a *story*, possibly one about an experience or incident that happened to us or someone we know? Well, it's this story that unconsciously communicates what we can't or are unwilling to say directly. It's our natural way of relating a story that will allow someone to know something we want him to know—without putting it to him straightaway. Maybe it's a personal viewpoint such as the way we're displeased at the mistreatment we feel the person suffers by another. Or it might be how we think someone should conduct herself. Whatever it is, not only is this road a socially appropriate and painless one, but through it, we don't risk the possibility of being taken the wrong way. Moreover, it allows us to be in rapport—even when we disagree with another's point of view.

Achieving rapport by playing back someone's strategy through a story is a natural dynamic of this communication process. It works because it makes use of an already established vehicle. It is unnoticeable by the conscious mind, yet is totally apparent and meaningful to the unconscious. What we are doing with strategies maximizes this phenomenon, charging common repartee with powerful energy that binds us to others through rapport.

We respond to storytelling because it speaks directly to our unconscious. If we build on this with new theories about communication, what we end up with is one hell of a potent mechanism for persuasion, influence, compliance, and rapport. Kind of a turbo-supercharged technology that speeds up the process as well as the delivery of "being on the same wavelength." It is incredibly simple and enchantingly effective, and is summarized by the following statement:

> *We engage rapport with someone by running his strategy within the same context, but with altered contents.*

Simply stated, we start and continue a "loop" of rapport by playing back someone's particular strategy for doing something. When we do this, however, *we must always change* the content around *the strategy* so that the conscious mind doesn't interfere with the process. What this means, quite simply, is to strictly follow the context of the strategy—in this particular case, A→K→V—*but* use new story content. It's like using the plot to *The Wizard of Oz*, but adding different dialogue. There's a whole long scientific explanation about this, having to do with what the mind will and will not accept. But what's really important for us to know here is that we always feed back to the mind the new story content wrapped around the context of the strategy. Let me give you that again:

Always feed back to the mind the new story content wrapped around the context of the strategy

---

This is a most natural chain of events. Like putting the right key in a matching lock. A perfect fit. Unchallenged and unqualified. The lock doesn't care where the key is made, who made it or what it looks like, so long as it fits perfectly. I can assure you this is so fluid a process that if you listen real closely, you'll actually hear the tumblers pop open!

Now we can apply our rapport-building skills and invoke the first law of strategies. To wit:

To be in a "real estate" selling rapport, we play back the buying strategy—with one additional element. *That element is a change in the* content *of the story.*

I would escort Mr. Smith to a piece of property that, of course, was as close to what he wanted as I could find. I would use his strategy, A→K→V, as a guide for knowing what he truly wanted—a place that *sounded* interesting enough to produce a *feeling* that in turn produced a pleasurable remembered *image*. And then I would implement the first law of strategic rapport: I would play back his strategy through a story with brand-new content.

I would walk him around the property and, *through storytelling*, offer back his strategy for buying real estate.

Package 1

"Well, Mr. Smith. How do you like it? Kind of nice, isn't it? You know, when I previewed this property for you, I could **hear** the **sounds** of yesterday as I walked through the house. Like I'd been here myself a long time ago. It's **funny** how a house will give you that **feeling.** I could **sense** that anyone living here would **feel warm** and **secure** in the fact that this home was a really good value. **Looking** at it from that **perspective**, you can probably **see** what I mean."

At this point, not only have I used the first law of strategies, but I'm fulfilling a basic rule of rapport: people like people who are like themselves. Smith's trust in me, not to mention his affinity for me, has just increased tenfold. You see, I'm being like him. I'm reminding him of himself. He's listening to me but hearing his own agenda for buying. After all, it's *his* strategy that I'm running back to him, isn't it? I'm fulfilling *his* requirements for satisfaction and delight in buying real estate.

I've simply followed Smith's buying strategy, A→K→V, by giving him an auditory representation first, a kinesthetic representation second, and finally a visual representation. The content of the story was almost incidental. All I did was use the context of A→K→V and added story content.

Sometimes, just one run-through will be sufficient to achieve rapport. On some occasions, though, you may have to repeat the strategy a few times. No big deal. You can replay the strategy as many times as you need to. Simply change the content each time. To illustrate this, let's "redesign" the content, run it by Mr. Smith, and then analyze it.

Package 2

"You know, Mr. Smith, when I was here the other day, I found some of that old-style barn-sided wood that was used for construction way back. The tone of those slats was remarkable. They could be hammered together with such clarity and were in such harmony with the outside design, it made me feel sorry for modern-day houses. They just don't fit homes like they used to. Kind of a lost art. When you look at something this pretty, you can really get a picture of framing it as your own."

Analysis

Auditory

"You know, Mr. Smith, when I was here the other day, I found some of that old-style barn-sided wood that was used for construction way back. The **tone** of those slats was remarkable. They could be **hammered** together with such **clarity** and were in such **harmony** with the outside design . . ."

Kinesthetic

". . . it made me **feel** sorry for modern-day houses. They just don't **fit** homes like they used to. Kind of a lost art. . . ."

Visual

"When you **look** at something this **pretty**, you can really get a **picture** of **framing** it as your own."

All I've done is code the content differently. It hardly makes a difference what you play back for Smith as long as it fits his strategy of A →K →V, and you give it to him in the precise syntax of his strategy.

When I began developing this technology, I'd practice with friends over dinner or while driving to the country—even on the tennis court. Why, I've had occasions when I've been with people where in the course of an hour or two I did nothing else but repackage and play back. After a while, most of what I played back was word salad. That's right. Totally meaningless nonsense sentences, placed within their strategy, for whatever it was I wanted to be in rapport with them about. You must remember that the verbal portion of communication accounts for only 7 percent of what's communicated. Tone of voice, body language, and context make up the remaining 93 percent. So go ahead and try this out for yourself. But you must have patience. Don't forget you're just getting your feet wet in a technology that will serve you successfully for a very long time. And nothing this good is learned completely overnight. Here, practice makes perfect; and like anything else, the more you practice, the better you get at forming instant rapport. I know it may sound simplistic to you at this point, but strategies are really quite easy to use once you learn what to do with them and how to play them. They really work.

For those of you who are still skeptical, and to achieve even further clarity, let's apply what we've learned to a strategy other than buying. All of the rules and principles of Mr. Smith's buying strategy will apply to this strategy as well. It's one that people request I demonstrate quite often in my seminars.

You're out with Scott, a really wonderful man you want to get to know. He's just your type and you sense that if you could get the chance to know him better, something nice might happen. Trouble is, this is where things usually fall apart. For a lot of reasons. Nervousness, anxiety, miscommunication—a whole raft of junk that gets in the way. What to do? Well, this is exactly where knowing another's strategy for attraction will drastically alter the outcome of the evening—for both of you.

My favorite environment for this kind of strategy engagement is a nice restaurant with a comfortable and appealing atmosphere, which adds to the effectiveness of total rapport. But it doesn't really matter where you go as long as you're able to talk peacefully with each other. And don't be heavy about all this. You're not performing surgery or speaking in public, and rapport establishment is not celestial mechanics. You're out to have a good time.

As the conversation turns to each other's past and you each begin to share personal history, bring him into state by asking the first strategy question.

1. Scott, can you remember a time when you were totally attracted to someone?

Remember what I've said about questions. You may very well use the ones I've outlined here. But always be appropriate to the situation. Obviously, you wouldn't want to state strategy questions in the same way as I have if you've just met this man. You might want to phrase it differently, such as expressing interest in what he's talking about. For example, when the subject of the opposite sex comes up, as it inevitably does, you might gently ask, in response to his description of someone:

"Were you attracted to her the moment you saw her?"

"What was it about her that was appealing?"

"Do you remember what it was about her that grabbed your attention?"

All of these questions are acceptable. Remember, you're simply trying to ascertain his first representation of her. Do what works. Those who have the widest choice of possible approaches will get the highest number of positive outcomes. This applies to all the questions in strategy unpacking.

In much the same way as we did with Mr. Smith, we're taking Scott back to a time when he experienced total rapport within a specific context. In this case, the context is attraction. He'll search his memory, attempting to locate a specific experience in which he was terribly attracted to another person. He might think of a former girlfriend or possibly of his first love; or maybe his memory will be of someone to whom he was very attracted but never got the chance to act on his feelings. Remember, the content of his memories really doesn't concern us. In fact, having the integrity to respect another's privacy is an important notion to embrace when building rapport with someone. Our concern is to get him into state; to have him get a clear experience of being totally attracted to someone.

Scott will access each step of his memories primarily through a visual process, or an auditory process, or a kinesthetic process. When he settles on a specific experience of being very attracted, he'll let us know verbally, "Okay . . . yeah . . . I remember," *and* by going into state with physiological manifestations such as a smile, a raised eyebrow, or other body language. Each person has his own way of showing when he's in state. Some people shift in their seats, others flush a little, maybe look down and to the right to access feelings about a memory; some people will get goosebumps on their forearms. Your instincts will inform you when someone goes into state. Trust your experience, and pay attention to how people respond to your questions.

When Scott ends his search and gets a clear experience of being totally attracted, he may or may not tell you of the memory. It matters not, for the next question will get him to respond not only with content but, more importantly through his sensory representational systems. If he wants to relay a story to you, as we have below, fine. Listen attentively, for it will add to your knowledge of him.

In response to your question: Scott, can you remember

a time when you were totally attracted to someone?, Scott may smile and say, "It's funny that you ask, because I automatically think of this person I knew a long time ago. She was my first girlfriend. I remember her so clearly, how interesting to think of her right now."

He's representing this experience to himself internally, and he's probably very much in state.

You're now ready for the next strategy question.

2. Scott, can you tell me the very *first* thing that caused you to be attracted? Was it

1. Something you *saw*? Or was it
2. Something you *heard*? Or
3. Something that *touched* you or that you *felt*?

Once again, by asking him to be sensory-specific, Scott's reply will naturally hand you the first step in his attraction strategy.

"How could I ever forget that? Jeez, it was the first time I was ever wild about someone, y'know? I can just **see** her now, right in my mind's **eye.** She was standing by the piano at my friend's house, talking to her friend Chris...."

"And the very first thing that attracted you was..." you say again.

"Oh yeah, for sure it was the way she **looked** leaning against that piano. Kind of like a life-sized **photograph.** It was unbelievable. I can just **picture** her now."

It's easy to see that Scott's first step in his attraction strategy is visual. When he thinks in terms of being attracted to someone, he makes a picture of the experience in his mind. He sees himself being attracted. His attraction strategy has been like this ever since his very first experience of being attracted to someone.

We'll represent his first strategy component with a **V** for visual.

3. Scott, after you saw her standing there by the piano, what was the very next thing you remember that attracted you? Was it

Something else you *saw*? Or
Something you *heard*? Or
Something that *touched* you or that you *felt*?

Again, what we've done is ask him to be sensory specific.

"Right after I saw her?" he replies.

"Yes, right after. The very next thing."

"Hmmmm..." He smiles and gets some color in his face. "I just **heard** this **voice** in my head **saying**, 'Boy, am I turned on to her.' It was **loud** and **clear**," he says, while looking to the lower left and rubbing his ear.

That was strategy step 2. The sight of her led him to an internal dialogue about his attraction. He could hear a voice validating the picture.

We'll represent this *internal* dialogue with an **A** for auditory. So far, then, we have:

$$V \rightarrow A$$

The next step is simply a repetition of the first two. We just plug in the information Scott supplies to us in the appropriate blanks, and feed him another sensory-based question.

4. Scott, after you *saw her standing by the piano* and *heard the dialogue inside*, what was the very next thing you remember that attracted you? Was it

1. Something else you *saw*? Or was it
2. Something else you *heard*? Or
3. Something that *touched* you or that you *felt*?

"There was nothing else after that. I mean, what more can I say?" he says, looking to the lower right. "I've told you everything I can remember. I saw her, told myself how incredible she was, and that's it. There are some things you just get a **feeling** about. I got that **feeling** in my stomach. You know when it's the real thing."

Deny it as he may, our friend actually has had a third representation. He got a feeling after the internal dialogue. The feeling of being attracted.

With this last representation of his strategy, kinesthesia, we have totally unpacked Scott's attraction strategy and can represent it, in toto, by: $V \rightarrow A \rightarrow K$.

Strategy Playback

Remembering that a good portion of establishing rapport has much to do with offering back someone's behavior, we may now begin to weave Scott a story that taps in to his attraction strategy. We base this methodology on the unconscious delight we experience when we're related to through metaphor.

Knowing Scott's attraction strategy, $V \rightarrow A \rightarrow K$, will allow us to tell him a story (content) around the framework (context) of his attraction formula, thereby causing him to be attracted. If we keep this in mind, and remember that we initiate rapport with someone by running his strategy but changing the content so as to bypass his consciousness, we'll find ourselves suddenly and miraculously rapport bound. In this example, since we're running Scott's *attraction* strategy, we'll find ourselves on the receiving end of a rapport that is based on the way Scott is wired up for attraction. In other words, Scott will suddenly feel irresistibly attracted to us. Don't be shocked when this happens. You see, it will be very hard for him to *not* be attracted because, just as we did in Mr. Smith's case, we're fulfilling a basic rule of rapport: people like people who are like themselves.

So far, we've unpacked Scott's attraction strategy by asking him about a time when he felt totally attracted to someone. In doing so, not only have we ascertained his personal formula, but we've increased our chances of rapport by expressing interest in Scott as a person with a unique past. You know, it's fascinating; we aren't really attracted to someone who's interest*ing*—no, not for the long haul; we're attracted to those who are interest*ed*. By using strategies, we place ourselves in the space of being interested, and by doing that we delightfully add to the probability and richness of rapport.

At this point, Scott is relatively receptive and is becoming interested in what you have to say. At an appropriate moment, maybe when the conversation has slowed down a tad and you look at each other and sense an openness and clarity, gently begin the story that will contain Scott's attraction strategy (V→A→K) and cause him to start feeling attracted—to you.

Package 1

"You know, Scott, judging from the way you describe her, your first girlfriend **looks** like she was a terrific person. It must have been an unbelievable **scene** meeting her that way. I can just **picture** you **looking** at this woman and **telling** yourself how attracted you are to her, much as you would to someone who you knew would be in **tune** with you. From the **tone** of your voice, it would be **safe** to **say** that you would be **excited** and **charmed**."

By the time you've completed the strategy, Scott will have changed. His perspective will definitely have been changed. His experience of you will be from the point of view of an altered state. Scott's attraction for you has either just kicked in or has been magnified greatly, because you are complying with the first rule of rapport: people like people who are like themselves. Don't you get it? Well, like whom do you think you're being? Whose ideal of attractiveness have you just become? That's right! You're being just like Scott, and are in an attraction rapport with him. You are reminding him of what attracts him to someone. He's listening to the story yet hearing the tumblers of his heart fall open for you. *He can't not be attracted at this point*. I mean after all, it's *his* attraction strategy you're running back to him, isn't it? You're fulfilling his requirements for being attracted.

The content of the story was almost incidental. All we did was use the context of V →A →K, and added story content.

This strategy may be replayed over and over simply by changing the content. I must warn you, though, that continual replaying will dramatically speed things up and you may suddenly find yourself in a situation that, to put it delicately, could place you in a compromising position. So be judicious and attentive to the response that you get. But just for the hell of it, let's do another "repackaging" so you'll get a good understanding of playing back a strategy.

Package 2

"Judging from your point of **view**, Scott, it **looks** to me like you can really **see** what attracts you to someone. I've had the same experience. Just **looking** at the right person will literally get my **bells** to **ring**. It sets a whole different **tone** to the day. It **tells** me, in a very **warm** way, that this person is **special** and gives me a **feeling** of butterflies in my stomach."

Easy, isn't it?

Again, we've followed V →A →K by giving Scott a visual representation first, then an auditory representation, and finally a kinesthetic representation, exactly as we did in the first package. The content of the repackage or second "version" was, and always will be, virtually irrelevant. We just used the context of V →A →K, and added story content. Remember to be judicious in replaying; I don't want you running off into the sunset—just yet!

Some of you might be wondering how strategies would come in handy at your job. Well, there's probably no other technology as powerful and persuasive as strategy unpacking and playback for getting results at the office! If you stop and think about it, knowing your boss's strategy for any particular task should be a very natural part of being in alignment with her. In fact, "misalignment" is what prevents us from maximizing our potential at the office.

When we know another's strategy for a specific behavior, doesn't it make sense that we'd be able to perfectly satisfy that behavior, if asked of us? Of course it would. But it's terribly difficult to satisfy another's behavior when we don't know her criteria for satisfaction. An example of this that we can all relate to are those times when we did just what our boss wanted us to do—and even got the result he wanted—but failed to please him or be acknowledged for it. Familiar? Think of all the times (and I'll bet there are quite a few) when you did exactly what was asked of you—even more than what was required—maybe even produced the outcome your boss wanted, only to fail at gaining your boss's favor. Even worse, someone else came along and did what you thought was a second-rate job but your boss became overwhelmed with delight! Remember how outraged you felt? And you had good reason to feel outraged. You *were* doing your best—it just wasn't good enough. But that's precisely the point. You were doing *your* best. Your boss wanted you to do *her* best. Running her strategy instead of your own means offering back to her exactly what she wants, without filtering it through your own head. It's a little like the George Burns/Gracie Allen routine. When they would end their show, Burns would say, "Say goodnight, Gracie." And Gracie would say, "Goodnight, Gracie." She was doing exactly what he said to do (offering back his strategy). If she had run it through her own strategy, she would have said goodnight to the audience.

Whether you're an executive, a lawyer, a secretary, in

middle management, a shopkeeper or a salesperson, or even a senior vice-president, if you're able to satisfy your boss's strategy for the work to which you've been assigned, the results you produce will be ten times more appealing and a hundred times more appreciated. So go ahead and ask your boss how you need to represent your work so as to produce the best results *for her.* Just remember to phrase your questions so that you get a sensory-based answer, such as the ones we've learned earlier in this chapter. So, if your boss asks you to have the Jones account ready for him to review by next week, you'd ask:

"Joan, have you ever had someone prepare an account for you just the way you wanted?" or: "Joan, did you ever know anyone who was the best at presenting account status? Maybe someone who made it real easy to get the details quick and effectively?"

Then watch her eye accessing cues, listen to her processing words, and observe the order of her representations. Believe me, she'll spell it right out for you. Sometimes you can see the whole strategy just by her eye cues alone. If she looks to the upper left, then the lower right, then the lower left, you'll know her strategy is V→K→A. So the first step in preparing the Jones account would be to make it strongly visual. In fact, you'd want to show her visually, through big column or pie charts or brightly colored storyboards, how well or how poorly the account is doing. This will satisfy the visual part—and step one—of her strategy. It'll produce a strong feeling within her about the account, thereby completing the kinesthetic part—and step two—of her strategy. Next, you'll want to explain verbally any data you think is appropriate, thus fulfilling the auditory—and final—part, which will complete her presentation strategy.

When you present the account, mirror your boss the entire time. In fact, while you're running her strategy, mirror the way she's sitting, the way her head is tilting, and the way she's using her hands. But remember, *don't mimic.*

When you're through with her strategy, continue being in rapport with her by using the same process words she does. If you sense that you want even more rapport, by all means repackage the story and run her presentation strategy again.

In the following chapter you'll learn about anchoring. With anchoring you'll be able to use the way your boss felt about something previously pleasing and successful, and have him transfer those feelings to you. When you fire off anchors while running his strategy, mirroring him, using his eye accessing cues, and matching his process words, how do you think your presentation of the Jones account will go? Do you think your boss will find it satisfying? Well, let me ask you this: whose behavior will he be judging? Why, his own, of course. What you've been doing all along is simply presenting the Jones account exactly the way your boss likes it presented and finds immensely satisfying.

You can apply strategy technology to *any* aspect of your working life. It doesn't have to remain a secret weapon you pull out only in emergencies.

If you want a raise, find out your boss's strategy for raise giving and run it back on her a few times. Use anchoring to associate a good feeling from the past while running this strategy.

If you want a promotion, elicit your boss's promotion strategy by asking her, maybe off-the-cuff, about a time she gave someone a promotion. Then continually run it when you're around her while mirroring her and anchoring her to a feeling of generosity. This will cut waiting time by months.

If you want to have the highest sales statistics in your firm, just consistently unpack your clients' buying strategies and make selling effortless.

Strategies are so totally effective because you're offering back to people their own secret formula for whatever it is you want. You're accessing their nervous systems and acquiring their blueprints for very exact models of behavior.

Don't forget you're asking them questions for very specific portions of their conduct. There's nothing general about strategy unpacking. It's very difficult for people to turn down their own formula for the way they behave. Can you recall an instance in your past where someone fulfilled all your criteria for something? Maybe it was a specific morning or evening your boyfriend did everything you desired— even things you didn't tell him to do. Or the time your daughter made you totally proud of her. How about when a project of yours ran absolutely perfectly—just the way you wanted it to? Didn't it just make you feel wonderful? Wouldn't you have done anything to reward everyone involved at that very minute? You bet. Do you know why? Because, quite unknowingly and by happenstance, those people involved tapped in to *your* strategy for whatever it was they were doing at that moment. Wouldn't it be nice if you could make your boss feel toward you the way you felt toward your boyfriend or girlfriend or kids or friends the day you just wanted to give them the world?

You can, through strategies.

Review

Strategy Unpacking

We elicit someone's strategy by getting him to slow down and replay for us a behavior we'd like to unravel. The way in which we get a person to do this is by asking certain specific questions about the strategy we're interested in acquiring. These questions are designed so that the person will express herself through her sensory representational systems; in other words, in terms of images (visual), words and sounds (auditory), and feelings or touch (kinesthesia). Following is a strategy questionnaire. Use it to acquire someone's strategy.

THE STRATEGY QUESTIONNAIRE

XXXXX'd = Behavior

Examples: attracted, satisfied, buying, creative, navigating, perfection, totally committed relationship, great sex, learned something totally, felt good about yourself, motivated, got up on time, et cetera.

1. Can you tell me (or remember) a time when you were very XXXXX'd?

2. Can you tell me the very *first* thing that made you XXXXX'd? Was it

- Something you *saw*? Or
- Something you *heard*? Or
- Something that *touched* you or that you *felt*?

3. After you (saw, heard, felt) XXXXX'd, what was the very next thing you remember that made you XXXXX'd? Was it

- Something (else) you *saw*? Or
- Something (else) you *heard*? Or
- Something (else) that *touched* you or that you *felt*?

4. After you (saw, heard, felt) XXXXX'd, and then (saw, heard, felt) XXXXX'd, what was the *very next thing* you remember that made you XXXXX'd? Was it

- Something (else) you *saw*? Or
- Something (else) you *heard*? Or
- Something (else) that *touched* you or that you *felt*?

For our purposes, learning the first three steps of someone's strategy is sufficient. The first question brings them into state, the next three unpack their strategy.

Strategy Playback

1. Start and continue a "loop" of rapport by playing back someone's strategy through a story.

2. Package the *content* of the strategy so that the conscious mind doesn't interfere with the process. Use the strategy as a context or "shell" around which to place a general story—*the content*. Repeat.

3. The strategy ("shell" or "context") *must be exact*— the content *un*familiar.

4. The content (story) can be in generalities.

5. Don't be cruel! Limit your replaying. You don't want to have the entire population of your town falling in love with you! Do you?

Stop! Take a breath...Relax.

You've just learned quite a lot. It's time to take it easy for a moment. I've given you an awful lot of material in this chapter. But don't be put off by the work. Strategies are worth the effort to learn, because once you've mastered the technology, you won't believe how your business and personal life will change. I can't emphasize enough how powerful you'll become.

Start out slowly just observing people and notice how they have definite steps they go through before completing specific tasks. Then, when you feel like a dry run, play around with the questions, and see for yourself how people represent experience. Before long, you'll want to dive in and do strategy unpacking. By all means, go ahead. Take your time and see what happens.

Remember, though—you're just starting out and might make a mistake or two at the beginning. You should've seen me when I first started. If you looked in the dictionary under the word *awkward*, you would have seen my picture. But in no time at all I was zipping along. I promise you that with a bit of work, you'll be able to gain mastery over this superlative technology and have it work outstandingly for you at home, at the office, and in all other areas of your life.

Now let's have dessert. Put on your wizard's hat and get a sorcerer's apprentice, because we're moving on to the magic of anchoring....

10

ANCHORING

YOU'VE had a disagreement.

Tempers flared, and for the last hour or two you've been sulking around the house feeling cranky and out of step. You really want to make up but just don't know how to get him to see your point of view. Tired of moping, you decide to try and open a dialogue even though you know it won't be easy. You walk into the den, where he's hunched over the desk finishing some work he's got to have ready for Monday. You know it's not the best time to ask him to talk, but you feel it's important to handle the situation now—not later. So you call, "Honey?" and stand there waiting for the worst. He looks up at you and, for no apparent reason, gives you that special wink he has, which you've always adored. Like a hand reaching into your very soul, you feel loved and secure again. All of your anger has vaporized, and you are once more connected. You're back in rapport.

You're in your boss's waiting room rereading the market survey that your team has developed and that you're going to present to him in about five minutes. You can't help but hear loud voices coming from behind closed doors and realize that the old man's giving someone the business. Your anxiety rises as the door opens and out walks the vice-president of your division looking disheveled and devastated. The secretary whispers, "It's been like this all day." You hear the buzzer on her desk, she motions you to enter, and you walk into his office upset that you haven't been given last rites. He's standing by the window, looking out, but turns as he hears you approach. You're so nervous you drop your portfolio, bend down to pick it up, and as you do you unwittingly mutter under your breath, "Jiminy Cricket." You straighten up to find the boss smiling whimsically. You're so flustered, you just smile back, hoping it's the right reaction. He proceeds to drop into his overstuffed chair, lets out a relieved sigh, and says, "I haven't heard that expression since I was a boy back in Carmel. You know, I remember a time..." You take a deep breath and slowly relax, knowing for sure what it must feel like to have nine lives. This meeting's going to be a piece of cake.

You're in bed with her and it's the first time. It's been six or seven months since you broke up with your ex and you've decided to take the plunge... again. Everything so far's been pretty dreadful, what with old memories stirred up and indecision about being with someone new—someone you're not even sure you're really turned on to. You're just about to pull up stakes and call it a night when she touches you in that exact spot with the exact pressure and in the same way as you know who. Suddenly you find it's totally okay to be there. You lie back with a quiet certainty while a voice deep within you says, "How wonderful to feel loved again."

What do these situations have in common? Well, for one thing, in all three something is happening to make either ourselves or the person we're interacting with behave in a way that's not expected. And something in each drama is eliciting behavior that has its roots in a past experience. Psychologists tell us that we're activating a stimulus-response reaction. Sociologists might say we're demonstrating operant conditioning. But as far as we're concerned, and for all those interested in establishing instant rapport, the common thread that's woven through all three scenarios is *anchoring*.

What is an anchor? Technically speaking, an anchor is a representation—either internal, as with a picture or feeling, or external, as with a touch or sound—that triggers (elicits) another such representation. It's a sensory stimulus paired with either a response or a specific set of responses or states.

Anchors are all around us—the sound of the doorbell at home, the smell of coffee at the office—even making love, with its myriad of personal anchors. Advertising is awash in anchors. What do you think of when you're watching television and hear the famous three chimes? NBC, of course. If I told you, "You deserve a break today," what would you think of? Would you get hungry? Just a little? Before advertising used anchors, if I told you that you deserved a break today, you'd probably agree and ask me to clean your house or maybe do your laundry.

The sound of church bells is a commanding anchor—we automatically feel reverence and faith. The sight of the American flag or the bald eagle is anchored to pride in our nation. When someone touches our hand, we reactivate the anchor of acceptance and warmth. Have you ever smelled an old book? Try it. It'll take you way back to your childhood. How about a song you shared with someone you loved? What do you think of when you hear it now? Anchors are powerfully effective. Any portion of a particular experience can be used as an anchor to access another portion of that experience.

I'm particularly susceptible to tonal or musical anchors. Because I'm auditory, I lock on to pitch and melody changes so overtly that the way I'm feeling can be totally shifted into another state just by my hearing a few bars of a song, or a moment or two of a concerto. Whenever I hear the theme from the movie *Marjorie Morningstar*, my **feeling state** and even my **physiology** are immediately changed. That melody is so anchored to the state of losing a love that it's almost impossible for me not to cry. This isn't the best anchor to have when you're out with the guys, by the way. But as a corollary, when my girlfriend called me "bummy"—a simple, ordinary word—it was such a powerful auditory anchor, linked to a state that was associated with loving her, that I knew she was feeling extra close to me at that moment. And this made me feel wonderfully high. Even intoxicated. Such is the power of anchors.

Anchors are somewhat different from stimulus-response mechanisms in that they don't require reinforcement or repetitive conditioning. In the stimulus-response model of learning, for example, each time a correct behavior is made by an individual, he is rewarded by reinforcement; e.g., a smile, praise, a pat on the back, and so on. Anchoring requires none of that. Behavior is created at the moment of anchor installation and really doesn't demand much of a reward and certainly no repetition. So it's entirely possible to anchor someone to a specific feeling state with what psychologists call one-trial learning. In other words, conditioning looks to repeat the desired behavior over and over in order to "burn" it in, while anchoring requires only one shot—one distinct, well-oiled volley—for installation. When we "install" an anchor we are metaphorically describing its placement.

In case you're wondering exactly how you would use an anchor to establish rapport, let me give you an example.

Once, I was going out with a terrific woman who was just lovely to be with, but who unfortunately enjoyed smoking. Well, there was no way I could hang out with her *and* her cigarette pack—one of us would have to go. I thought this might be a good time to use an anchor.

One evening she was explaining how very upset she was when she had been fired. I asked her to elaborate on it and encouraged her, gently, then not so gently, to get back into the feeling of letdown and rejection. Now, I wasn't being a sadist here. I simply wanted her to step into the negative experience of rejection, so that I could use this state to anchor her away from smoking. You see, there are only two rules for anchoring, and one of them is to make sure that whoever you want to anchor is as much in state as possible.

> Being in state means duplicating a specific feeling *now*, at the moment or height of a particular experience that occurred in the past, *then*.

To put someone in a state of anxiety in order to build an anchor; so that we can associate smoking with anxiety, for example, we would either wait for him to be in that state spontaneously, or induce the anxiety by asking him to recall a time in his life when he was in a highly anxious state. We create anchors when we're in an intense state—one in which both the body and mind are in total alignment and total congruency. In much the same way as we did with strategy unpacking, we'd ask the person to get really in touch with how he felt when he was anxious. We'd encourage him to experience the anxiety *visually* by asking, "What did you **see** that made you so anxious?"; and *auditorily* by asking, "Was there something you **heard** or something that someone **said** to you that made you anxious?"; and also *kinesthetically*, "Did someone **touch** you or did you just get a **feeling** of anxiety deep within you?" The person doesn't have to answer with the content of what caused the anxiety. In fact, that's almost unimportant. The point is to get him to step into the *state* of anxiety you want him to have, so that you may install an effective and powerful anchor to it. Anxiety, of course, is just one state you may use to associate an anchor to. Can you think of a good reason to anchor someone to a pleasant state? Of course you can. If you want someone to have all her resources for, let's say, success available to her when she goes for that important job interview, you'd anchor her to a state of success. And just like anchoring to anxiety, you'd want to make sure that the recall of *this* state is as vivid and as real as possible for her. So you'd ask the same questions to stimulate success, representationally, as you did for anxiety. You can always tell from people's nonverbal behavior when they're in state. Remember the expression on your face and how you felt when you got that raise, or that date you wanted, or the time you were fired, or the state you were in while on Space Mountain at Disneyland? How about when you got an A+ on that paper you worked so hard on? You were very much in state then. That's what we're looking to re-create when applying or installing an anchor.

When we anchor a person to a particular state, then, the information that's recalled by him when we trigger that anchor at a later time is contextual. That means that the feeling state (of joy, happiness, success, lust, rejection, sadness, or anything else) is what's recalled—*not* the actual content or event. So when you fire off an anchor paired with joy, for example, the person you've anchored to it will reexperience the joy but not the particular experience that caused the joy. This is absolutely terrific because it allows us to create a raw feeling and then associate it with any anchor we choose. If we've anchored someone to joy with a short abrupt cough, for example, he will become joyful. Period. We needn't be concerned with joy as it pertains to a specific experience in his past. What this sets us up for is the ability to create joy and have it, via anchor, *associated with us.* If we've anchored our boss to joy, and we fire off that anchor as we're presenting our point of view to him, what do you think will happen? He'll experience joy! He may not jump up and down and click his heels in ecstasy, but you can be assured that whatever you're saying to him, at this point, will be experienced through the filter of joy. That's the beauty of anchors. We take a feeling state out of someone's past and anchor it to a present situation.

So here I am, out on the town with this lovely smoker, attempting to arouse and augment her recent rejection and patiently waiting for her to be fully associated to it. When I was satisfied that she was in state—and I can tell you she was, because her eyes watered and she hunched over the table in the classic loser's posture—I placed my hand on her shoulder and squeezed, gently but definitely. I also leaned close to her and frowned right in her face while telling her, "That's terrible." She agreed, and told me, through her misery, how nice she thought it was that I truly understood. I thought the only thing that was nice was the anchor I had just installed. And it was. Because from then on, every time she lit a cigarette, I fired off the same anchor. I would squeeze her shoulder, frown, and look at her cigarette while saying, "That's terrible." Her unconscious mind paired the present stimulus of the squeeze (a kinesthetic anchor), the frown (a visual anchor), and the words (an auditory anchor) to the past state of rejection, which in turn created an unpleasant anchor in the present. In a short time, she generalized this redundant triple anchor to just the frown on my face. Instead of smoking, she got slightly upset— upset enough to make the experience of smoking feel lousy. That was the end of my problem—and of her smoking, at least when she was out with me. Sometime later, though, during the course of a phone conversation, she casually mentioned that she'd given up smoking. She said it just wasn't pleasurable anymore. I smiled.

I tell you this story as a demonstration of the power of anchors. Not only do they allow us to support positive behaviors in others, but they immeasurably assist us in establishing rapport. Of course, you can use anchors for anything. In fact, most of the negative behaviors that couples maintain within their relationships are almost exclusively anchors. Unfortunately, one anchor fires off another, so what you end up with during a fight is two people relating to each other through their anchors. It happens to all of us, and it can begin for no apparent reason. You may look at her in a specific way that reminds her of a look she got in the past (maybe from you) that she has associated with upset, and she *gets* upset. She says, "What's the problem?" and that fires off your anchor associated with the boss because that's the tone of voice he uses. You look down or turn away as a response to that anchor, which fires off her anchor of rejection, installed years ago by her mother. She starts to cry, firing off your anchor of guilt, which was installed by your first girlfriend fifteen years ago, and which you don't know how to deal with. And so on. Sometimes we end up going to bed mad, hoping that by morning our psyches will repress these lousy feelings. And sometimes they do. Sometimes.

But anchors can also help to change all that. Do you know how easy it is to anchor someone to a wonderful feeling? It is nothing more than designing a trigger *now* to elicit a feeling that occurred *then*. Anchoring people to any feeling is ridiculously easy yet very effective. But before we talk about actual technique, I'd like to familiarize you with the two conditions that are absolutely necessary to create and install an effective anchor.

Condition I: Intensity of State

Probably the most important part of anchoring, either of oneself or another, is the *state* we're in at the moment the anchor is installed or put in place. This state is important because anchors depend on *intensity of feeling* to be effective.

The more intense or real the feeling state is at the moment of installation, the easier it will be to trigger the anchor response at a later time.

Since we're going to use anchors to create rapport, we want to make sure that when we install an anchor it is as fully associated as possible. When an anchor is associated, it is tied to a specific experience. Intensity of feeling is the single most powerful parameter of anchoring in this regard. If, for example, we want to anchor someone to be motivated, we'll want to make sure that she's totally associated to an experience she's had in which she was absolutely and clearly motivated. Encouraging her while in this process is vital. And it's easy to do. Just keep directing her to stay in touch with her sensory experience via sight, hearing, and feelings. People must have strong associations about the state you want to anchor them to.

Let me give you an example of anchoring in your life. I want you to fully relax for a moment. Dim the lights; get comfortable, and follow along. There's just one ground rule: take your time, go slowly, and try to re-create the experience as I describe it. If you can get a friend to read you the following process, it will work a thousand percent more effectively.

I want you to recall a time you were really happy. Not just la-de-da happy, but ecstatically happy. I want you to take a moment and try to get as much recall as you possibly can about this time. It may have been with someone you love or a particular place you visited, even a specific state of mind you once experienced. As you recall this time, what did it look like? What color was it? Was it bright or dark? I want you to see it as clearly as possible.

Good.

Now as you continue to think about this incredibly happy time, start to hear what it sounded like. Was it by the beach with the sound of the waves? Was it in the park, with birds chirping and children playing? Was there any music? Maybe there was a particular song you associate with this time. If so, let it play along in your mind. Relax. Let yourself go wherever the music takes you.

Wonderful.

What did this happy time smell like? Popcorn? Cotton candy? Chocolate? How about Italian food or antique shops? Did it smell of brand-new sheets or salty air? Was there cologne or perfume in the breeze?

Can you taste this happy time? Were there flavors you can recall? Were they minty or spicy? Can you associate the taste of fruity wine with this happiness? Sure you can. Does the taste of bubble gum bring back these moments of joy, of fondness?

Now really step into this experience. Take your time. Be back there, being happy. Can you feel the wave of happiness flow over you? Yes, I know. From the tips of your toes to the top of your head, you can bask in the delight of this special time. Mmmmmm. Wonderful. Now, relax. Take a deep breath and relax.

Relax...

Yes, that's it. Relax. I'll bet it's a joy to be so happy. Can you see yourself being this happy? I can. What a terrific smile there is across your face. A smile that say's "I'm really happy. I could stay like this forever." Can you hear the soothing memories bubble up through your mind like a brook in the forest? Naturally. Can you taste the lipstick you had on—whether your own, or that of your lover? Remember how it smelled? Those were happy times.

Great.

Now place your right index finger on your right temple and press gently for five seconds.

Thanks.

You've just installed an anchor—a wonderful anchor that can be used later as a refresher when you need the resource of happiness in your life. At the end of this chapter you'll trigger this anchor, and depending on how fully associated to happiness you just were, you'll re-create the sense of joy you just experienced. I promise.

Condition II: Anchor Placement

Now that we're clear about the importance of intensity of state while anchoring, let's take a look at the other critical requirement of a well-formed anchor: *placement.*

Obviously, you don't want to place an anchor in an area of the body that is used all the time. Handshakes and the like are poor anchors because they're constantly being triggered. Not only will this produce the anchor response on totally inappropriate occasions, but it will extinguish the response, over time, through exhaustion. Touching someone on the shoulder, which is a kinesthetic anchor because it involves touch, is okay, but other people may fire off the anchor inadvertently in the course of daily activities. The same holds true for common sounds (auditory anchors) and everyday visual anchors. In other words, if you're anchoring someone kinesthetically and have a choice of installing the anchor through a touch of the shoulder or, say, a squeeze of the ring finger, you'll create a more effective response with the less obvious finger anchor. This follows with visual anchors and auditory anchors as well. However, because kinesthetic anchors are so strongly wired into our feeling states, they have a slightly higher degree of effectiveness. So if you do have a choice, try and use a kinesthetic anchor—if not by itself then combined with other anchors. You'll find they will serve you well.

One of the techniques I recommend highly is the use of additive anchors. Simply put, additive anchoring, or redundant anchoring, is anchoring someone in more than one representational system at the same time. In the example about the woman who smoked, I anchored her in all three representational systems. I told her. "That's terrible," (an auditory anchor) while squeezing her shoulder (a kinesthetic anchor), and frowning (a visual anchor). These anchors tend to stay in place longer and are more effective because you're utilizing representations in all three areas of experience.

Random Anchoring

Random anchoring is just a fancy way of describing the process by which anchoring is accomplished through the spontaneous occurrence of intense emotion. This is the lazy man's anchoring system, and, of course, my very favorite. It's my favorite because it requires the least effort and is often very powerful. In fact, I use this with my friends all the time, often telling them what I'm doing. You see, anchors are so effective that you don't have to be covert about using them. I just wait until one of my friends gets excited about something and simply place an anchor on that feeling to be used later. Sometimes he'll say to me, "I know, you've just anchored me," and I nod in agreement. The funny part is that even though a portion of his consciousness is aware of the anchor, it doesn't lessen its effectiveness. That's what random anchoring is about. Maybe it would be better to call it "opportunity" anchoring. Let me give you an example.

About an hour ago my friend Steven called, really excited about a new client. He was literally beaming over the phone about it. I didn't need to encourage his enthusiasm, so I just cheered him on as he vividly described the way this client was going to lead to another, who would be even more profitable, and then still another, and so on. At one point he must have been moving along at the speed of light, so animated was he about the whole affair. Not one to let an opportunity go by, while he was positively bursting with enthusiasm, I gave a high-pitched, short, but *very* audible whistle. It interrupted him momentarily, but he didn't stop long enough to catch his breath and ask me why I had done that. Well, this auditory anchor is going to come in pretty handy tonight when we have dinner with Steven and his wife and his wife's parents, whom he's never very thrilled to be with. You see, that was his other reason for calling: he thought it would help him to have my moral support tonight. So you know what I'm going to do over dinner, don't you? At the lowest point of the meal, maybe when he's feeling really defeatist and bored with the company, I'm going to fire off that anchor of excitement and enthusiasm. Now, I don't know if it will improve the overall context of the relationship he has with his in-laws, but I will say this. First, Steven will be so enthused and excited that he won't give a damn and secondly, I think positive, good feelings are contagious, and if he's thrilled and delighted—even if he doesn't know why—I'm sure it will spill over to the others and provide an up-tempo framework to get all of us through the evening. I mean, people respond better to someone alive and inspired than someone hunched over his plate acting the brave soldier about to be shot. Have I got your interest?

Induced Anchoring

Random or opportunity anchoring makes good sense. But what if we have a specific purpose for our anchor or want to install an anchor and haven't got the time to wait for someone to go into state spontaneously? Good question. And a very easy answer. All we do is create that state by asking the person literally to re-create a specific experience. A terrific demonstration of this is the handshake that David Letterman uses when he closes a spot with a guest. Often, the celebrity doesn't realize the interview is over and sits there starry-eyed, absorbed in something else, as Letterman offers his hand. This can be ungainly for a host, as sitting there with one's hand extended waiting for a handshake is awkward. So Letterman, being a visual, uses this fabulous anchor of looking at his extended hand until the guest is forced to follow Letterman's line of sight, if only to see what he's looking at. When the guest's eyes catch Letterman's extended hand in front of him, it fires off an anchor of handshake. The guest has no choice but to accept the gesture, thereby allowing Letterman to close the spot and go to commercial. This is one kind of induced anchoring. Let me give you another example.

About a year ago, my best friend and I were camping out—really having a terrific time—when he confided in me that he was crazy about a woman whom he had started dating the month before. I slapped him on the back, laughing all the while, sharing with him how great that was; how I thought he really deserved to have love in his life. But his expression was incongruent with his words. When I asked him about that, he confided that there was a small problem. Though he was in love with her, she didn't feel the same about him. It seemed she had recently broken up with her boyfriend and was coming along okay, but would lapse into states of missing him—often when she and my friend were alone together.

"We'll be out someplace when she gets this soft look in her eyes and the corners of her mouth turn up like she's in total bliss," he explained, "and I know that she's remembering him."

Though she feels guilty about it, she told him that it couldn't be helped; that it happens like this once in a while, where she gets this warm toasty feeling from the past. Now this wasn't something terrible or that made her a bad person; in fact it spoke quite loudly of her sensitivity. But my friend was bummed out about it, and it was beginning to interfere with whatever intimacy they had.

I sat him down on a huge rock that bordered the stream we camped by, and for the next half hour I taught him how to take these wonderful feelings she had and not only make them productive, but channel them—yep, you guessed it—to him.

About three days later, I got a call from him in my office. He was ecstatic. He could barely contain himself. Talking—halfway stuttering—he called me a sorcerer, then told me, "I used that anchoring whatever-you-call-it on Christy. I can't believe it! It worked as though I cast a spell on her! She's really come around. When we walk, she puts her arm around me; when we watch the sunsets, she's really there with *me*."

I asked him how he had anchored her.

"Well, we were out at the beach, kind of napping— really in a terribly romantic state of mind—she in hers, back in the past again, and me in mine. But this time I didn't care. I just enjoyed the peace and quiet and content-ment that being with her always brings me. Then I asked her to tell me what it was like being in such a blissful state. Well, though she was surprised that I wanted to know about this, she really got into it. You know, she's one of those people who really get descriptive and animated.

"I took my time and waited till she was, ah—what did you call it?—fully associated. Then when she was just in heaven, I playfully grabbed both her arms by the wrists, gently squeezed, and went 'mmmmmm.' We both laughed. For different reasons. She, because I was acting cute and funny; me, because I was nervous wondering if the anchor would work. Then the craziest thing happened. About an hour later we were going to the market—you know, very casual and everything—when I took her by the arms again and squeezed her wrists and went 'mmmmmm.' But instead of laughing, she pulled away from me and got that look on her face: you know, the one she got when she thought of her old boyfriend. That's when I wanted to kill you. Man, you were a goner. I figured I had made things worse. Then out of the blue she moved very close to me, stood up on her tiptoes, leaned over my shoulder and whispered in my ear, 'You mean so much to me.' I thought I'd died and gone to heaven."

"For the last three days now, every once in a while I fire off the old anchor just to make sure everything's okay. It's really unbelievable, Michael, how she goes right into state. The same state as before, except it's with me. Once, over the phone, all I did was the 'mmmmmm,' and she called me sweetheart! I just can't believe it."

So their love life started as a function of her warm feelings of a remembered winter, and blossomed into a spring of rebirth.

Anchors are a fabulous tool we can use to access pleasurable states.

Let's review the steps necessary for a successful anchor.

1. Intensity of State.

This is very important as the response of your anchor will depend heavily on how associated the subject is to the experience you're anchoring them to. In random anchoring, waiting for the state to occur naturally is fine. With induced anchoring though, you must encourage the subject to relate back to a specific experience and nudge them into fully re-creating it. *The stronger the state—the more intense their experience as a result of recovering their previous feelings—the better your anchor will work when fired off.*

2. Placement.

Don't get careless and lose a terrific opportunity by installing an anchor with a weak placement point. Be creative. Remember, when using covert anchors, the person you're anchoring won't attach meaning to what you're doing. So what feels to you like inept groping will likely go unnoticed by him or her. And when possible, go for the kinesthetic anchor; it will produce the best results. However, when social constraints prevent the use of touch, you'll find visual and auditory anchors work beautifully, especially when they're installed simultaneously.

Combining Anchoring with Eye Accessing Cues

Eye cues will invaluably assist you in determining when a person is in state. You may install an anchor when a particular eye cue appears. For instance, if it's important that your boss get a picture of what you're explaining to her, ask her if she can picture what you mean. When she does, and her eyes move to the upper left or right, indicating that she is, in effect, picturing what you're talking about, anchor her to that behavior by installing an appropriate anchor. By the way, if she's still not getting the picture, direct her attention to her upper left by moving your hand up there via pointing to something on the wall or playing with your hair, or even looking to her upper left (your upper right). Then, as soon as she does, install the anchor. You might light a cigarette or light your lighter; you can sharply change the tone of your voice; or you can kinesthetically anchor her with a touch of some sort, if that's possible. If you follow the rules of anchoring, it'll be no sweat to elicit that same "picture-seeing" behavior when you need to again, simply by firing off the anchor you've installed. Honest.

Combining Anchoring with Strategies

Anchors are a terrific help when running someone's strategy for ... anything. Let's say you've determined that Mr. Jones's strategy for public speaking is A→A→K. You know that to speak effectively in public, Jones does the following, in this order:

1. *(Auditory)* Hears the words in his mind, then
2. *(Auditory)* Hears himself saying the words, and then
3. *(Kinesthetic)* Gets a feeling of correctness.

Jones is your boss, so when he presents an address to a few hundred of the company employees, you know that if he looks good, you look good. So you've been playing back his strategy for terrific public speaking the last five minutes or so, and he's ready to give a powerful speech. How about anchoring him to a time when he brought the house down with an inspiring and successful public address? Ask him to tell you about that time, encourage him to get excited, then when he's in that state, anchor him with an auditory anchor—in this case, maybe the sound of your applauding him. If you install this anchor successfully, what do you think will happen when he's introduced and hears the applause? That's right! His successful public speaking anchor will be triggered and he'll give 'em hell! Can you tell me a better way of getting promoted?

As you've probably guessed by now, anchoring yourself to resourceful situations makes wonderful sense. Do you think there are specific resourceful states of mind you'd like to be in from time to time? Me too. So what I do is recall a time when I've been deeply associated to an experience that

I consider resourceful and that is appropriate to what I want to create at the moment. Sometimes this is confidence or self assurance; sometimes it might be a particular state of happiness or bliss I experienced. Why, I've even used anchoring as an outstanding tool for losing weight! One time I used anchoring to overcome my fear of flying, and it worked so well I went on to take flying lessons! The point is, you can anchor anything. Well, once I know what I want to anchor, then I really step into that particular state, recalling what it looked like, what words or conversations were involved (both internally and externally), and what my feelings were at the time. Then when I'm really into it— totally and intensely associated to it—I install a personal anchor. Pow! Instantly, I'm charged with those resources I wanted. Now, when a situation arises where I need this resource, I simply trigger the installed anchor and allow myself to enjoy what I've wired in. Sort of like eating your cake and having it too! Anchoring and anchoring with strategies or eye accessing cues is like having it all. It is powerfully effective because it combines two singularly wonderful rapport-technologies and teams them together synergistically to create unlimited power!

Combining Anchoring with Language

Words are pretty strong anchors. Profanity is an example of this. No matter what state we're in, hearing a real gutter word will take us directly into a different mood. Well, any word can serve as an anchor. Very much like in trance work or hypnosis, words can cause real mood changes. If you'd like to use language as an anchor, just remember that words create pictures, sounds, and feelings. So when you bring someone into state and are ready for installation, use a word that corresponds with the function of the anchor. For example, if you're anchoring someone to playing a great game of tennis, and have gotten her in state by asking her to recall a time she played tennis effortlessly and creamed the competition, using word anchors such as "Game! Set! Match!", et cetera, will cause a picture of winning tennis to dance in her head. Or it will cause her to hear the crack of a perfect serve. Or it will create a winning feeling. Whichever way your partner represents winning tennis in her experience, you've empowered her with a cutting edge, simply with the use of an anchor. Of course, the reverse is true as well. I've had a few matches where I (dare I say this?) anchored my opponent to his worst defeat ever! I just felt awful as I collected my winnings. Eventually though, I became philosophical about it all and I recalled what Woody Allen once observed when he said that playing to audiences who were stoned didn't count because they'd laugh anyway.

Anchoring works!

Oh, by the way—touch your right index finger to your right temple. Mmmmmmmmmmm. Now, isn't that just terrific?

11

SEXUAL RAPPORT

HERE'S an interesting notion flying around out there—probably attached to the concept that opposites attract—that while rapport may be an important part of the social package, in the bedroom it's...well...irrelevant.

But, when we're out of sexual rapport, that part of our life is empty. You can readily observe this in others just by listening to everyday conversation. When women talk with other women, what do you hear? That her lover is the most exciting and considerate man she ever met? That she feels truly connected to him? That sex has taken on a new dimension in her relationship? Not really. Usually, it's quite the opposite. Her lover is too rough and insensitive; he's inconsiderate; when they enter the bedroom he becomes either a wimp or a madman and she absolutely doesn't know who he is when the lights are out. And she's probably right. She doesn't know who he is because between them, all sexual rapport is in absentia.

Last year, I invited a few friends out to the beach, where I live in the summer. One night, as we all retired, I remember being aware of the state of mind we were all in and couldn't help but notice one particular couple holding hands as they found their way upstairs to their room. These are good friends of mine, and I paused for a moment to think how long I've known them and some of the experiences we've shared over the years. Not long afterward, we all retired.

Somewhere about two A.M. , I awakened to the sound of moving furniture and loud whispers. It sounded like there was a meeting of the Teamsters downstairs. I got to the balcony and almost began my way down the staircase before I realized the raucous sounds were emanating from this particular couple's room. It was unbelievable. They were so blasé about their relationship when the sun was up, yet at night, it seemed they couldn't keep their hands off each other. I smiled, got back into bed, and after some strategic soundproofing, fell asleep. The next morning, we all had brunch out on the deck. But there was a difference in the air. And that difference was a noticeable break in the rapport of this very same couple. She had already talked to my girlfriend privately, and he took me aside a few minutes before heading back to New York. What he told me was something I've heard so many times before: He loves her, wants to make her happy, couldn't think of life without her—yet in bed they just couldn't get it together. It just wasn't happening. With all the techniques they tried—even pretending they were the Flying Wallendas—the bottom line in their sex life was one of tremendous effort that produced negligible results. And my girlfriend had heard pretty much the same thing from her friend. Was I surprised? No way. In fact, this kind of sexual disenchantment has become epidemic these days. When sex is good, it accounts for only 10 percent of a relationship's consciousness; but when it's bad, it consumes 90 percent of the relationship's survival.

One would think that fulfilling sex should be a natural and complementary part of a communicative and intimate relationship. But it just doesn't work out that way. So what's going on here, anyway?

You see, without sexual rapport, without that which makes all behavior cohesive and congruent, what's left is our archetypical and oftentimes inappropriately raw sexual response. We value this raw response as being something natural and attractive—even "earthy," if you will. We place a premium on those who exude it. We indulge this kinesthetic attribute as though it were a quality one should seek in life. The joke is, of course, that raw or human sexual response is something we—all of us—are born with! But we try to look like the Marlboro man and the Lauren woman to become exact personifications of sexual fantasy. And I use the word *fantasy* because we have about as much rapport with our sexual beliefs as we do with the IRS. So we've set up a situation in which what we get is incongruent or incompatible with what we actually desire. You see, we want intimacy. We want a relationship, we want to connect with another self. But what we go after is some specter, some made-up conglomeration of shimmering facts that has left us, as a society, sexually rapportless.

Sex requires its own set of rules and conditions for success. And I mean *success*—not *work*, for if *work* were the case, as a species we wouldn't be concerned with how it subjectively felt. And making matters even more complicated, sex needs to be rewarding not just for both together but for each as an individual. How can two autonomous adults, with different needs and wants, come together in a sexual union that is not only satisfying but also compelling? How can we get what we want while being the fulfillment of another's sexual ideal? Well, the answer goes beyond any sex manuals you may have read, any consultation you may have obtained, and any advice you've gotten over the telephone at one A.M. It goes beyond thinking of sex as this "thing" we do. It even transcends the pleasure principle. But "good sex," as Dr. Ruth calls it, is as close to your relationship as your own backyard. It's always been there. But like opportunity, rapport-rich sex is something you must create.

Creating Something from Nothing

Sexual rapport has two parts. First, we create it in our stream of consciousness. Second, we create it out in the world. That is to say that before we use the technology of rapport on the outside, we must create what our sexual experience is going to be like right in our own minds. If you doubt this, consider the following.

We create experience at two distinct logical levels. The first level, or "first attention," is the creation of a desired experience within the context of one's own mind. This never fails to occur, but we rarely have awareness of it because we're not conditioned to associate to it. But it is there. More than that, it's necessary. Let me give you some examples. If you're building an automobile, you strive to hammer down each and every detail of design before even going near a factory. You might consider if it's going to become a sports car or sedan; if it will be fast or slow; what kind of seats and windows it will have. Will it be an all-terrain vehicle or just a highway cruiser?

Suppose you were planning a company outing. Would you just show up at some isolated field with a sandwich or two you bought along the way? Would you tell other people how to get there? Would you check the weather forecast the day before?

If you were building your dream house in the country, would you consider which bedroom would go where? How many square feet do you want the house to be? Where and how big do you want the kitchen to be? Would the house be in New York or Utah?

Some of these questions might seem very basic. But, when we think more consciously, they push us to consider detail. The more detail we think of, the better handle we have on what we create in the world. What I want you to come away with here is that we create "out there" based upon what we do "in here." For everything.

The concept of "second attention" or "out there" is that before we manifest an experience in the physical world, we must clearly construct it inside. To the degree that we make it real down to each nut and bolt is wholly analogous to how successful, rewarding, and pleasurable an experience will be. Indeed, creating at the logical level of first attention is really everything. Without this awareness, we are out of rapport. But specifically, if we don't raise our sexual consciousness and—more to the point—if we don't create rapport within the context of our sexual lives, all of us will be doomed to scenarios just like that of my two friends, above.

The Strategies of Sexual Rapport

As I've outlined in chapter 9, everyone has a strategy or specific behavior for accomplishing singular tasks. We expanded on just two of these strategies in that chapter, namely buying and attraction. Well, sexual strategies fit very neatly into the same blueprint. As far as human behavior is concerned, a strategy is a strategy is a strategy. That means that any behavior follows more or less the same sort of formula of any other behavior. To put it another way, we elicit and play back someone's sexual strategy in just about the same way that we'd elicit and play back someone's golf strategy, or public speaking strategy, or attraction strategy. You see, what they all have in common is that they are behaviors. And behaviors always contain predictable representations that lead to the fulfillment of their outcome. If someone's buying behavior or strategy is **A →V →A**, for example, you can have a high confidence level that it will remain **A →V →A** for life. That's just the way it is. If their strategy for humor is **V →A →K**, you can make book that that's the way to make them laugh—eternally. Whether you like it or not, we're very much like machines in this sense. Press the right button and get the corresponding response. Forever. The mind is a stack of representations—and representations of representations—that are pictures, dialogues, and feeling states of successive moments of now. Let me give you that again:

The mind is a stack of representations—and representations of representations—that are pictures, dialogues, and feeling states of successive moments of now.

Now, let's get specific. While acquiring someone's strategy for business or social reasons supports the use of the strategy elicitation questions I've outlined in chapter 9, there are some obvious reasons why this procedure may not be appropriate for sexual rapport. That's not to say they can't be used, just that there's a more subtle and efficient method for obtaining a sexual strategy. And this is the use of eye accessing cues as a feedback mechanism for strategy acquisition. So, when you want to find out what another's strategy is for unbelievable sex, simply pose one question that will elicit the entire sexual strategy. But before you do, it's important to remember that this person be fully associated to the state you want. That is to say, since you're searching for a deep feeling state, it's necessary to have that person somewhat approximating that state of sexuality while you elicit their strategy. Now this is something that you can do in many ways. You can simply wait until it spontaneously happens; you can cause it to happen by leading the conversation toward sexual content; you may even wait until you're actually in bed with this person. Remember, this is not an attraction strategy you're running. That was outlined in the chapter on strategies. This is the strategy you run for terrific sex. And that means you've already established an attraction rapport with whomever you're considering having sex with.

So, you're with this really terrific person who totally turns you on, and you've led the conversation to the sexual theater, or done whatever is necessary to bring this person to be in as much an associated state of sexuality as possible, and you're ready to acquire their strategy. Great. Now, either conversationally or directly, ask them a single strategy elicitation question:

Can you remember a time when you really had terrific sex?

Remember that the question need only capture the gist of this basic sentence. And also keep in mind that it's posed in only the most appropriate situations. For instance, it might be asked over an intimate dinner as the subject of sex naturally surfaces. Or, it might be posed while actually in bed, while gently caressing each other. It could even conceivably be asked during a business meeting—so long as the person you're communicating this to is in the same space, and as fully and sexually associated, as you. At this point, it's all about appropriateness. And remember that the question can be syntactically structured in many variations. For example:

In response to a train of thought:

So, it was really that great? Hmmm...and you can remember it that clearly? Or No, what do you mean "great in bed"? Was it that unbelievable? Or Tell me what you mean by that. I can't imagine it being that outrageous.

What I'm trying to get you to see here is that the content of the question isn't that important at all. It's the context that makes the difference. It's just being able to get that person fully associated to a state of high sexual response. You might try repeating a question or pursuing a line of thought until you observe the response you want. Once you get it, you're ready to read eye accessing cues.

This is the easiest part of the deal. What most people get hung up with here is the basic skills of eye access cue interpretation. So before continuing, go back to chapter 7 and give it another look-see, then return here and we'll move on.

The wonderful thing about someone's eye cues is that they are totally reflexive, outside their conscious attention, yet they can instantly reveal any strategy. So as soon as you ask a sexual question of someone who's in a fully associated sexual state, watch their eyes and you will observe their exact strategy for what they consider great sex to be. It's up to you, then, to take that strategy and play it back so that it produces sexual rapport.

In response to your strategy question, if someone looks lower right, then lower left, then lower right again, what does that tell you? Very clearly, it should tell you they:

1: Are experiencing a feeling.

2: Are telling themself something about the feeling.

3: Are getting another feeling, possibly about what they just said to themself.

Another way of describing this is:

$$K \rightarrow A \rightarrow K$$

FEELING $\rightarrow$ DIALOGUE $\rightarrow$ FEELING

The eyes will always give, in order, the representations of the sexual strategy. It's up to you to observe it and play it back. If you didn't get it the first time, relax. Simply replay the question and watch where your friend's eyes travel. Once you get the hang of it, it'll become second nature.

Now we know *what* will bring your friend into sexual rapport. The next thing we want to do is *use* the formula of $K \rightarrow A \rightarrow K$ to activate his sexual response. You may do this in many ways. You can use metaphor—that is, tell a story using the $K \rightarrow A \rightarrow K$ formula as a shell within which to place the story—or you may act out your behavior in such a way as to be sexually enticing while heavily charging the situation with your friend's specific sexual strategy. It's even more effective to do both. For example, you might put your arms around this person, gently whisper into her ear, and then stroke her hair. That's acting out $K \rightarrow A \rightarrow K$. Of course, what you'll say in her ear is a $K \rightarrow A \rightarrow K$ formula: I feel so good when I'm around you, I can hear bells ringing and I feel warm all over.

A fellow psychologist friend of mine, who happens to be dating a brilliant and nice looking but sexually unmotivated woman, recently called to share with me his "unskilled" (his word, not mine) use of sexual rapport technology. I'd like to pass a part of our conversation along to you.

"...the interesting thing was that I entered into this situation heavily doubting her attraction for me. It's not that she was uninterested, it's just that she had this middle west value thing that was truly blocking her, in a sexual sense. And I know from my own clinical practice that the longer this went on, the less probable it would be that we'd have anything even resembling a normal sex life.

"Anyway, the last time we went out I was so crazed with her that I figured I might as well try anything. We went to dinner, and then back to her place for coffee. Instead of having to beat around the bush, I just waited until anything regarding sex came up, then asked her about it. When I noticed she was there—right there—I casually inquired about what she thought made terrific sex. She smiled a little then proceeded to give me this discourse on what the place would look like and that she had seen it in a movie, and remembered how much the music moved her and so on. So later on, when I kissed her, I told her that she looked like she belonged in a picture frame, and how I wish we were in that picture together, and how cute I thought she looked the day I met her, and then I told her a few explicitly personal words that normally I would have felt funny saying, but that I knew would turn her on. She became quite receptive. But the best part was when we were in bed. I followed the same formula while actually having sex—you know, $V \rightarrow V \rightarrow A$—and it brought her so high, I couldn't believe this was the same down-home woman I had been seeing all this time. In fact, following this strategy in whatever I sexually did was simply irresistible to her—even stuff that *I* initially felt uncomfortable with—making the sex we had that night just fabulous."

When you create sexual rapport, what you're essentially doing is making it safe and comfortable for others to express themselves openly in a sexual setting. Moreover though, by completing another's neurological circuit, by setting up a mirror image of them on a highly unconscious level, you're running their own behavioral blueprint for whatever it is they consider great sex to be. It may not be a particular sexual act, nor a specific sexual event, but that has little to do with rapport. You see, through rapport, the space becomes open and clean enough for your partner or yourself to communicate what it is they really want. Think about that. You may even begin to see that in its own way, it's logical. I mean, how many times have you been in bed—in this theater of alleged intimacy—and felt inhibited about communicating to your lover exactly what you want? Isn't it weird that while you're entrusting your body to someone in its naked vulnerability, at the same time you're unable to simply say, "Here's what gets me crazy"? Of course it is. So establishing rapport simply makes good sense. For both people. If a pilot doesn't understand what the navigator is saying, do you really think they'll get to where they both want to go? Please.

Anchoring Pleasure

While you're thinking about that, let's not forget how valuable anchoring is to great sex. In fact, you might say that anchoring is your insurance policy to continuing what strategy playback has begun. If you're like me, you don't want to have to keep running someone's sex strategy over and over. Why manually shift when there's automatic drive? You already know about anchoring and how it creates previous states of behavior in the present. Well, it just so happens that anchoring someone's sex strategy or anchoring someone's sexual response is easy, very effective, and fun. And, of course, it works.

Here's how to do it. When you've acquired someone's sex strategy, or have brought them into a sexual state, anchor them. It's simply too good an opportunity to waste. As you remember, you may anchor someone either visually, auditorally, or kinesthetically. Anchoring can be made even more effective by redundancy, that is to say, anchoring in more than one representational system at a time. My favorite is combining talking and touch. When I bring someone into sexual rapport, I always anchor them with a specific word said with a particular sound while touching their body in just the right place. This works unbelievably well. A full explanation of anchoring technology can be found in chapter 10.

Sexual anchors are inherently powerful in any representational system because of the nature of the behavior being anchored. For instance, firing off a whispered auditory anchor whenever you lean over your lover and say something is an extremely effective way to bring him into sexual rapport. In fact, because whispering simply communicates raw sound, you may embed any suggestions or commands within the context of the whisper. So once you've initially placed or installed an anchor to a state of high sexual excitement with an auditory whisper, you may, thereafter, insert any words you want *into* the whisper. The possibilities, of course, are endless. Once you've installed the anchor, you then have it available to you as a resource state, which you may call up at any time. Hopefully, in the right situations. I don't think I need to tell you how compromising it can be to fire off someone's sexual anchor in the wrong situation. Which leads me to remind you to make sure you install anchors so that they won't be inadvertently reactivated by someone else. Right here you can see that handshakes, laughing, and obvious hand signals are out.

Mirroring

Mirroring is such a powerful technique, we have to be discreet in its use in everyday life, but in sexual rapport we are free to use its incredible power. It will increase your levels of sexual rapport a hundred fold. If you mirror your lover, what you'll achieve is not only a highly significant merging of physiology, but mental synergy that will enhance sex in a way you've probably only dreamed of.

A tremendous part of sexual chemistry, and the most powerful mirroring tool, is breathing rhythm. I cannot tell you how important and integral breathing patterns are to sexual rapport. When you match the respirations of your lover, you bring him into an altered state of consciousness that is not only very very heady, but opens up a pathway for suggestion that is highly influential because of its ability to persuade. You see, sex is located almost exclusively in the mind, and since we know from our definition of the mind that it is a stack of multisensory representations, we can create or enhance sexual reality and fantasy simply by coming into sync with our lover's breathing. Does this mean we must breathe the same way and in the same rhythm as our partner? Of course not. If we did that we'd probably hyperventilate, and that would defeat our primary objective, since we'd be passed out on the floor. But we can directly mirror breathing for *brief* moments in time. And when we break free of these moments, we may continue the pace by placing our sexual movements in the same rhythm. If you make love to the rhythm of your lover's breathing, you'll create a deep sexual rapport. If your movements correspond to the cadence of your lover's inhales and exhales, you'll be able to provide exactly what your lover wants. And when you feel tired, switch into another representational area by . . . let's say . . . stroking her hair (kinesthetic pacing), or maybe visual pacing by alternating your facial expressions. Also, don't forget the other sexual rapport technologies you've learned. And be bold. Try using them together—what I call *layering*. Anchor highly erotic states. Play back sexual strategies while mirroring breathing; anchor orgasms to a specific personal sound. You see, most of the time, your lover isn't *really* concerned with *what* you do, or even *how* you do it, so much as if you're both on the same train heading for the same destination. It's always infinitely easier to ride the horse in the direction he's going.

The best way to sexually travel is, of course, together. But it's even more important to let yourself go wherever the music takes you. With that thought in mind, what I've given you in this chapter is a technology that provides a way for taking your lover along with you, no matter where it is you want to travel. It is, I assure you, a safe context in which to either create sexuality in your life or to greatly enhance it within the parameters of your relationship.

In sex, being on the same wavelength is everything. When you pace your lover's breathing, you literally create wavelength after wavelength of pleasure. Now, in physics, this is called quantum theory. But in bed, it's called sexual rapport.

CONCLUSION

Once upon a time there was a famous medicine man in Northern Canada who was said to have enormous powers. When he waved a blanket at the northern lights they changed color. Every time he waved the blanket, the northern lights really would change color.

One day, he lost his blanket, and the northern lights changed color anyway. That ruined his reputation as a medicine man.

Life, without rapport, cares about you pretty much the same way as the northern lights cared about the medicine man. Struggling to get life to work is like waving your blanket at the sky. No matter what you do, life turns out in the same rapportless way as it always did.

Now, if you're willing to have rapport in your life, and willing to learn the technology that brings about rapport, there's no doubt that life will respond with an equal measure of rapport. In effect, life will mirror your output of rapport. In doing so, your ability to produce results—both in your personal relationships and in your business affairs—will be greatly transformed.

In order for us to get results, it's absolutely necessary that we be able to fulfill *others'* criteria of satisfaction—if we even dare to aspire to have them cooperate in our own agendas. The very best way to accomplish this is to care enough about our communication with others to ensure that it's clean and easily understandable. When you stop and think about it for a moment, all people really want is to be understood. Totally. When people sense that you understand them, that you really experience the reality of a given situation much as they do, it makes it safe for them; it becomes okay for them to allow their most prized personal signature—their point of view—to be altered. In this way we can get others to align themselves with *our* purpose, which is to produce results in *our* lives. And in doing so, we create rapport.

> You either have *results*, or the *reasons* you don't
> have results.

Rapport relies heavily on aligning ourselves with others' strategies. When we want to get a result in our lives as a benefit of another's cooperation, we need simply to find out what strategy that other person uses for the result we want. Given the technology we've just learned, this task becomes a guileless, unconstrained, natural process. The really nifty part about it, though, is that by achieving our goals, we satisfy those who've become part of the program. That's why when we run other people's strategies to gain value, all parties profit.

One can readily see how this applies at the political level. Ronald Reagan was a president who fully understood the relevance of rapport. In fact, his presidency succeeded in large measure as a result of his personal charismatic power. He knew that to mold and shape our nation the way *he* saw fit would require efforts that neither Congress nor the populace would find desirable. But he accomplished it, for the most part, with relative ease. Reagan knew that if he were in rapport with the people, the people would support him—even if they disagreed with him in principle. That's why when he needed to get a particularly important result, he would run the content of *his* thoughts and ideas through to the Congress and the public, using our contexts for listening to them and understanding their meaning. In his fifth presidential year, an independent study revealed that if they could, a vast majority of the voting public would designate Ronald Reagan president *for life*. What other president could have endured the scandals of Reagan's last two years in office—with people openly and harshly critical of him—while maintaining an affectionate rapport with the public? Though we made jokes about him and dismissed some of his later acts as inept, we enjoyed him; we saw things through his frame of reference because in more than one way he reminded us of ourselves. We even called him the Great Communicator. To this day, the Gipper's Teflon presidency—though criticized for mistakes in foreign policy and laissez-faire management—is remembered more for his ability to get us to like and support him than for anything else. Moreover, because of his skilled use of rapport, the distant future will come retrospectively to analyze the Reagan years as a time of unity and support between government and the governed.

Business relationships, like political and personal relationships, are functions of rapport—the more of it one can generate, the greater the chances of positive outcomes. Communication synergy between salesperson and prospect will reflect the seller's ability to establish high rapport. Like a presidency, where the relationship is between one person and hundreds of millions, and a personal relationship, which often is between just two people—the success of any business relationship is based on understanding and trust. Rapport is that vehicle which allows these two conditions to bear fruit. The higher and richer the level of rapport, the more satisfactory and productive the relationship between seller and buyer. When we observe a company whose sales curve is moving downward, we're almost always observing a company whose rapport with its buyers has declined.

You now have the technology and the wherewithal to create instant and deep rapport in your life. Practice what you've learned until it becomes fluid and charged with your own personality. Don't impose restrictions on yourself by sticking only to the examples I've given you. Try to expand the technologies and methods you've learned by constantly stretching and reaching for new levels of rapport. If you set about the task of applying the skills of rapport-technology to life as you live it day by day, you'll actually notice a major shift not only in the quality of your communication but within the context of your relationships. You see, the meaning of your communication is the response that you get! So, in many ways, the quality of your life is the quality of your communication. You *are* your communication, both in how you communicate with yourself and how you communicate with others.

Do yourself a favor. When you finish reading this book, don't stack it on the bookcase! Instead, read it again. Concentrate fully on each chapter. Really learn the technologies as best you can. You'll know you're really learning the material if you find the book worn and dog-eared after a few months. Many of you came looking for that elusive quality of magic that would transform your relationships forever. Well, your search has brought you here. Take advantage of the beauty you're being offered. You may have just found your heart's content. Don't let go of it so easily.

You know how we go through life—and this applies especially to our relationships—always holding back a percentage of ourselves for the next big hit—if it comes along?

We hold back just enough of ourselves that we don't get *totally* involved, just in case. For example, if we meet someone we're really nuts about—someone who adds immeasurably to the quality of our lives—we still keep 20 percent in the old silver box, just in case it doesn't work out or someone even better comes along. Well, for once in your life, surrender. Let go. I promise I won't laugh at you if you make some mistakes as you learn about rapport. Give rapport-technology all of yourself. Become totally committed to having rapport in your life and making your relationships work. Dive into the technology; immerse yourself in it. Teach it to your friends and family. Let people know you're involved and care enough about them to want to improve your abilities and the quality of your interactions. If you have considerations and judgments about the validity and credibility of this technology—continue to have them. I'm not asking you to give them up—it would be a shock to your system if you did, anyway! But just for once, let them be there and forge ahead in spite of them. Give yourself a break. If, after committing yourself to this technology—studying it, learning it, using it, and sharing it—you want to toss it aside, feel free to do so. That's your right. But at least give yourself a chance. I mean, if you're going to look for another way to effect change, what else will you look for? Isn't rapport the missing link? Doesn't it make sense?

IF YOU ALWAYS DO
WHAT YOU'VE ALWAYS DONE
THEN YOU'LL ALWAYS GET
WHAT YOU'VE ALWAYS GOT

Do you know what a gluon is? It's an extraordinarily small subatomic particle. It was named "gluon" because it holds together the other subatomic particles such as positrons and mesons. In a sense, it's the glue of life itself. Well, rapport is akin to a gluon. At the heart of all true relationships, there's rapport. Without it, we fall apart; with it, we're related. Can you think of someone whose life is rich with quality, but who's not in rapport with others? I doubt it. Even people whom we dislike and are not in rapport with *are* in rapport with those in their life they consider worthwhile. There's no getting around it. If you want to be successful at your life's work; if you want to have powerful personal relationships with others; if you want to be in a meaningful, long-lasting relationship with someone special—you must be able to create and maintain rapport. The first move in grasping the notion of rapport is to put down your blanket.

I'd like to leave you with this. The technology of rapport is a model and should be treated as such. Never let it, or anything else, dictate who you are. And when you're clear about its function, when you've become a soldier of aliveness, what you'll have left, and what you'll discover about yourself, is that when you're in rapport with life, your life is filled with love. Remember: a heart is not judged by how much it loves, but by how much it's loved by others.

Godspeed.

To communicate with the author,
and to inquire about consultation
as well as audiotape, videotape and
corporate in-house training, address
your queries to:

MICHAEL BROOKS & ASSOCIATES
P.O. BOX 191
PALISADES, NEW YORK 10964

To communicate with the author, and to inquire about consultation as well as audiotape, videotape and corporate in-house training, address your queries to:

MICHAEL BROOKS & ASSOCIATES
P.O. BOX 191
PALISADES, NEW YORK 10964